The
BONE LADY

The BONE LADY

Life Lessons Learned as One of
Football's Ultimate Fans

DEBRA DARNALL

a.k.a. The Bone Lady

GRAY & COMPANY PUBLISHERS
CLEVELAND

Gray & Company, Publishers
www.grayco.com

ISBN: 978-1-938441-53-0
Printed in the United States of America

1

For my beloved dog Molly, who taught me what real love is and how to love without condition.

Love never dies.

A friend once said about my dog Molly, upon meeting her and noticing she had one ear up and one ear down, "Well, she'll never win Best of Show!" I took that as a compliment. Her uniqueness is what I loved most about her.

"Do not go where the path may lead, go instead where there is no path and leave a trail."

—Ralph Waldo Emerson

Contents

Preface

This book is about more than football. Sure, I'm telling you stories of my adventures as an ultimate football fan of the Cleveland Browns—the ups, the downs, the good, the bad, and the ugly. But I'm also inviting you into other parts of my life. I created the Bone Lady character out of my passion for football and the Browns. I did it for fun, never thinking it would change my life. But it did.

As it turns out, my journey as the Bone Lady has really been about discovering who I am and why I'm on the Earth. Now, I'm sharing that story to help inspire other people to overcome the fear of being who you really are.

Just before sitting down to write this, I learned that a dynamic, charismatic, handsome young man I knew had died of a heroin overdose. I had met him only once, but for a guy at the beginning of adulthood he had made quite an impression on me. He had a spark about him, and I could see what a huge light he was in the world. How tragic that he couldn't see it for himself.

I believe we all come to this planet knowing who we are, but after we arrive many of us forget. Our culture conditions many of us to think we're not good enough, that we have to prove our worth. We fall into the trap of defining ourselves by external influences—jobs, relationships, religion, family, material possessions, our appearance, accomplishments, and accolades. Slowly we get farther and farther away from our true self. The next thing we know is that we have lost any sense of who we are and why we're here.

Thanks to the Bone Lady, I've learned that it's possible to regain that sense. It's ironic, I know, that when I put on a costume I finally learned how to just be myself. But that's what happened. It made me realize that whatever you love or love to do, that can be your calling, a path you can travel throughout life. In my case, it just happened to start with a beehive wig and a Bonemobile. Who knows what it will be for you?

Once while shopping in a grocery store I saw a small toddler sitting in a cart. As I walked by she blurted out very loudly to the world, "I am so happy!" The other shoppers never even looked up, but I got the biggest grin on my face. I thought, Wow, what pure spirit! Now I realize the key is keeping that pure spirit, that joy, throughout a whole life's journey.

Be light, be love, and be who you are!
With gratitude and so much love,
Debra (Bone), a.k.a. The Bone Lady
GO BROWNS!

Football Happens,
Life Goes On

Late morning on the Sunday after Thanksgiving of 2000, the day before my mom's funeral, I arrived at Billows Funeral home with my live-together boyfriend Tom (there needs to be a better combination of words to describe our twelve-year relationship). Walking in the back door, we were immediately greeted by the funeral director, who was expecting us. After exchanging pleasantries, he turned and said, "Well, here it is!" He gestured toward a casket as if he were Vanna White displaying a vowel. Setting down my box of paints and drop cloths, I stared at the casket and asked, tongue in cheek, "Uh, she's not in there, is she?"

"No!" he blurted, not aware that I was joking. He then told us to make ourselves at home and asked if we needed anything else. "No thank you," I said, "I think we're good." I looked over at Tom who nodded in agreement. Mr. Funeral Director started to walk away then paused, turned around and said, "Oh and one more thing: all I ask is that you don't wander around the funeral home."

I stood there a little stunned, wondering if now I was the one missing the joke. Wander around? Are you kidding? Tom and

I assured him that we wouldn't. He walked away and we both laughed. The thought of exploring a funeral home, opening doors to rooms where dead bodies were probably lying on tables, had never occurred to us.

Tom unfolded the drop cloths we'd brought with us and laid them out on the floor around the edges of the casket. I unpacked my paints and brushes.

Mom was the one who had started me on my art career journey. If it hadn't been for her suggesting that I paint for others, and opening doors by introducing me to colleagues through her antique business, I never would have become an artist at all. At the time of her death, I had been making my living for the previous fifteen years traveling the country as an itinerant artist, painting nineteenth-century-style landscape murals. My work was featured in national decorating magazines.

Mom had been my biggest advocate. So when she had approached the end of her struggle against colon cancer, I told her that I was going to paint a mural on her casket as a tribute to her life and a thank you for all she had done for me. Mom had always joked, "I just want to be buried in a pine box." When my brother, sister, and I had to pick out the casket, we learned that a pine box is not an option in this day and age. We settled for the simplest one they had. When I asked the funeral director if I could paint it, he said, "Hey, once you buy it, it's yours to do with you want."

I started sanding away on the lid and sides of the box. Next I primed the whole thing, and while that was drying I mixed up the tan ochre base color. Mom had loved objects with an old patina on them, and she loved my little cedar trees. I used sepia tones with raw and burnt umber to paint striped hills with those little trees lining their tops along the base of the casket. I painted a big heart on the lid, along with a weeping willow—a symbol of mourning.

When it was almost time for the Browns game to start, Tom went out to the car to get our radio. While he was gone, the owners of the funeral home, a nice older couple, came in. They said they wanted to meet me—no one had ever requested to paint a casket before. I explained why I was doing it and thanked them for taking the time to stop by. The woman commented on how much I looked like my mother. "Oh, thank you," I said. "So you knew her?" Immediately I realized my mistake. She had never met my mom but had seen her downstairs lying on a table. Duh!

As I worked, my mind kept flashing back to my childhood, things Mom would say and do, and how much she loved it when, as an adult, I would come for a visit. We'd sit in tall, straight-backed, gray linen chairs in her living room, talking for hours. Those chairs were so uncomfortable, but we hardly noticed. We'd get lost in our conversation.

I wasn't paying much attention to the sound of the Browns game on the radio until the sudden excitement in the announcer's voice snapped me out of my memories. I found myself quickly getting caught up in the game. Tom was, too. As the Browns were getting closer to scoring, we both started quietly chanting, "Go, go, go!" with our voices unintentionally crescendoing louder, louder, and louder! Suddenly, Mr. Funeral Director popped his head around the corner and sternly asked us to keep it down—there was a funeral going on in the next room! We abruptly stopped cheering, like kids reprimanded at school. But as soon as the funeral director disappeared again, Tom and I had to struggle to keep ourselves composed. Our laughter was like hiccups that we were desperately trying to hold in! Mom would have loved it.

I don't remember if the Browns won the game that day or not. It's all still a blur. I do recall, however, the strange experience of being behind the scenes of the inner workings of a funeral home. But most of all I remember the feeling I had while creating something so meaningful at a time when I had lost the most important person in my life. No one loves you in the same way that your mom does. She was the one person I could go to no matter how bad things got in my life or how much I screwed up. Mom always had my back. On that day, the activity of painting her casket gave me a way to celebrate her life and the years that I'd had with her. Not only was that nurturing for me, it helped start my process of grieving and healing my loss. Instead of crying my five hundredth millionth tear, drowning in my sadness by mourning her death, I rejoiced in her life. Who knew that a Browns game would become a beautiful Divine Distraction?

Mom was still on my mind two weeks later when I spent the entire day celebrating in a different way with my other family, my fellow Browns fans. That orange-and-brown-wearing family didn't know anything about my personal loss, about my mom's long battle with cancer, or any of the other turmoil unfolding in my life. Yet being with them became a sort of cure for my heart. They say laughter is the best medicine, and for a few hours on a Sunday afternoon, being the Bone Lady helped me to heal.

I am Debra Darnall, a.k.a. the Bone Lady, and this is my story.

Everything Begins
with a Thought

In November 1995, Cleveland Browns owner Art Modell dropped the bombshell, announcing that he would relocate the team to Baltimore for the following season. That episode has been written about extensively, so I won't go into it here except to say that, like all fans, I was devastated by it. A feeling of powerlessness engulfed me. This historic, iconic football team—our team—was woven deeply into the identity of Cleveland and the hearts of its fans, but none of that seemed to matter. Business was being conducted, they were leaving, and no one was stopping them.

A few months later, the NFL announced that the Browns would stay in Cleveland—sort of. Modell was awarded a new franchise in Baltimore, and the Browns were to be "deactivated" until 1999, when a new Cleveland Browns team would take the field with the same colors, records, and history. This helped ease the pain, but it still meant no NFL football in Cleveland for three years. It still felt horribly unfair.

The only thing that I could control was how I responded, and I chose to not watch one NFL game, not even the Super Bowl, until my beloved Brownies returned home. For three long years

I did not waver in my conviction. I was living in Columbus at the time, so I did watch a lot of Ohio State football. The Buckeyes are like a pro team in that town! So those games gave me my football fix. Plus, the Cleveland Indians were doing well, making it easy to get swept up in Tribe fever.

In February of 1999, the NFL held an expansion draft, allowing the new Browns to select players from other teams to begin building their roster. These were players the other teams had left unprotected, so they weren't exactly all-stars, but for the first time, the Browns' return to Cleveland felt real! There was a flurry of news and buzz about our Browns, and I got really excited.

So excited, in fact, that one morning I woke up and announced to Tom that I was going to paint my car like a Browns helmet and put an eight-foot-long bone on top.

Tom just looked at me curiously and said, "Okay?" He was used to my creative impulses and usually went along with them. I was always doing things around the house like repainting walls several times, moving furniture to different rooms, digging up plants in the yard. Once I even had this urge to cover the woodwork in the living room of our Arts and Crafts–style house with pistachio nuts. Only after experimenting on small wooden objects first, and attracting an infestation of little bugs, did I concede that this probably wasn't a very good idea. But it would've looked awesome!

My determination to paint my Volvo wagon, however, was unwavering. This voice inside my head was like a mysterious power calling me to action. So when friends and neighbors heard my idea and told me I was crazy, I didn't listen to them. Their negative comments rolled past my ears like jumbled jargon; I couldn't even comprehend a word they were saying. They asked, "Why are you doing this?" or "How much money is this costing?"—but I heard, "Blah, blah, blah." I was a warrior on a mission and having a ball! Fortunately, Tom was supportive and soon enthusiastically joined me in the fun of transforming my car.

The first thing I did was purchase another used Volvo to use as my regular car. Then I had my 1987 Volvo 240 wagon professionally painted to look like a Browns helmet. The guy who painted it loved my idea and even made me a face mask for the front of it out of PVC pipe. Tom helped me design and engineer the neon-lit bone for the top of the car while I proceeded to work on the interior.

During the day, Hannah, who worked for me on art projects, helped me with some of the grunt work, then at 7:05 in the evening I'd pop a cold one, climb into my car with glue gun in hand, turn on the radio, and listen to Tom Hamilton call the Tribe game while I glued every Browns-related object I could find to the inside of my car. I covered every inch with Browns newspaper and magazine articles, Browns memorabilia, and Dawg Pound paraphernalia—which served as a sort of Browns-themed wallpaper. I adorned the front seats with Dawg Pound jerseys. I found Browns fabric to cover the door panels, then stapled ball fringe for a border.

I covered the wagon floor with green felt like a football field and then filled it with all kinds of Browns and football memorabilia, including an Elvis lamp (rumor has it he was a Browns fan!). Then I proceeded to cover the dashboard with toy footballs, little dog statues, trophy replicas, and the largest collection of rubber dog poop ever assembled on a car dashboard. You name it, and if it related to the Browns, football, or dogs, I had it in my car. Even my license plate said "WER BACK"!

I also installed a killer sound system and had a bone flag made, along with flagpoles, for tailgating. The bone on top was made out of white plastic with orange lettering that read "Bone-mobile," and when you plugged the cord into the lighter socket, it glowed white neon. I had a horn hooked up that barked like a dog.

*   *   *

Being a little obsessive, I gave myself a deadline and signed up to participate in the Doo Dah Parade on the Fourth of July. Founded in Pasadena, California as a satirical counterpart to the Rose Bowl Parade, and now replicated around the country, the Doo Dah parade is all about being outrageous and having fun, making it a perfect place to debut the Bonemobile. The day before the event, during a cookout with the family and friends I'd recruited to be part of the "Bone Brigade," I set to work assembling the elements of a costume that I'd been gathering. Soon, the Bone Lady was born.

I had already dyed an old shirt tangerine orange and had made a skirt. I took those into the garage with my glue gun and started gluing my dog Molly's Milkbone dog biscuits all over them. (To this day, when people ask how the Bone Lady was created, I always say, "This is what happens when you drink too much beer and own a glue gun!")

I spray-painted a Marge Simpson-style wig that I'd purchased at The Yankee Trader, an old novelty store on High Street in downtown Columbus. That's where I also had found much of the paraphernalia for the car's interior, and where I bought 1950s-style sunglasses, bone-shaped earrings, and other items to glue onto my wig. And it's where another customer, a well-known drag queen in town, explained how to make my skirt stick out. "Hula hoop, honey!"

I glued letters onto my white velvet evening gloves, spelling out "bone" on one arm and "lady" on the other. On the chest of my shirt I spelled out "BONE IT," a play on the Nike slogan "just do it." I then spray-painted my navy blue 1970s platform shoes bright white and dyed a recently purchased pair of white fishnet stockings orange. The last item to my outfit, the pièce de résistance, was a pair of orange biker shorts that said "Art Sucks" on the rear. The last three years of waiting for our team to come back and the disruption and heartbreak that man had caused was a fresh wound, so I guess I was looking for a way of expressing my displeasure with what he had done. What better way than a message on my ass!

The Doo Dah Parade was a blast. My friends walked in front of the car, carrying a "Bone Brigade" banner and throwing candy. Another friend drove the Bonemobile and I walked behind, waving and flipping up my hooped skirt to moon the spectators with my "Art Sucks" shorts. The crowd cheered, barked, and laughed hysterically, as if my mooning action was some sort of cathartic medicine and they all had taken the pill.

In August, on the Thursday before the first preseason Browns game, I drove my Bonemobile north, traveling up Interstate 71 from Columbus to Cleveland. I stopped in Medina to have dinner at my cousin's restaurant, Main Street Cafe on the square. When I came out and got in my car to leave, there was a note on the windshield: "We love your car! Call us ASAP Fox8 news."

I called and told them that I was staying at my sister's house in Richfield and that I hadn't driven to Cleveland yet. They wanted to follow and film me driving into the city. Being the ornery person that I am, I said, "Oh, and I have this little outfit that I wear!" So the next morning they met me at my sister's, followed me up to Cleveland, filmed me on the way in to town and also in the Flats, the popular nightlife district not far from the stadium. It took most of the morning, and when we were finished, a massive pep rally for the Browns was under way on Public Square. Still in my Bone Lady garb, I walked over to the square with my dog Molly leading the way. As soon as I walked into the crowd, I was swarmed by the media like flies on you know what! Then, a woman from Continental Airlines grabbed me and led me up on stage, where I proceed to moon the city of Cleveland and the Browns players who were sitting behind me! They all cracked up! That woman who took me up on stage would end up being one of my dearest friends.

After an exciting day, I was exhausted and headed back to my brother's apartment in Ohio City. We watched my story on Fox 8's six o'clock newscast and laughed about everything that had happened. I'd had my fifteen minutes of fame and that was nice but the game was tomorrow and we were pumped up for it!

The next morning I awoke very early to a phone call from my mom. She wanted to tell me that there was a huge picture of me on the front page of *The Plain Dealer*. When my artwork had been featured in decorating magazines, she'd never made a big deal about that, but this had made an impression! I thanked her for calling, but that day I was focused on the game and still had no clue just how far all of this would go.

We packed up our tailgating gear, I put on my Bone Lady outfit, and we headed off to the city's municipal parking lot near the new Browns stadium to party and celebrate before the game. People started pulling their vehicles into the Muni lot over the course of the afternoon. Since it was a night game, the lot gradually filled up with tailgaters and families. It certainly wasn't the crazy scene the Muni lot would become known for in later years, but that afternoon was the most surreal, out-of-body experience I'd ever had. All day, people approached me, and they all knew the Bone Lady's name—just one day after my first appearance in Cleveland! Later I learned that CNN had picked up my story and had played it all day on Headline News.

It wasn't like I had been doing this for years, paying my dues and trying to make it happen. This new persona took on a life of its own right out of the starting gate. It felt like destiny was unfolding and I was just a passenger. I was just having fun, trying to make people laugh with my outfit and my car. Little did I know that I was about to embark on the wildest ride of my life!

"WER BACK" and the Bone Lady Ride Begins!

Driving up from Columbus to Cleveland in the Bonemobile with my dog Molly, Tom and I would go to Browns games. We would sometimes drive up the night before, staying at my brother's, sister's, or mom's house. We had tickets with my brother and his wife. That first season, fans were so full of excitement that the Browns were back and there was a special positive energy in the air. We weren't so concerned with winning because we were football-starved and just happy to have our team back.

Tailgating was not only fun, it was a spectacle, with fans from all walks of life. Some had also painted their vehicles. Many set up tailgate camps with tents and Browns flags waving on tall poles, devoting the whole day to grilling, playing cornhole, throwing a football, eating all kinds of food, hearing all sorts of music, dancing on top of RVs and buses, visiting with old friends, making new ones, and celebrating that our Browns were finally back. That phrase "Browns fans never lose a party" was never so true.

Game days were like a major holiday celebration, with all of the fanfare and decorative festivities. I was too young to have experienced Woodstock, but judging from accounts of people who were there and from documentaries, it was similar in a way to our tailgate experience every Sunday. Instead of music, we gathered to revel in the game of football and our Browns. Every week, fans got more creative with expressing their deep connection to the team. People who during the week worked very structured jobs were let loose and free to be themselves in the parking lot on a Sunday morning. It was all about having fun. We didn't really expect the team to win, at least not right away. But as the years went by and losing became the norm, "Thank God for tailgating!" became our mantra. We couldn't control what happened on the field, but we could create our tailgate party however we wanted. Each year, the parking lots seemed to overflow with more and more Browns fans painting their vehicles and adorning themselves in team colors.

We would pull into the Muni lot around six a.m. to claim our spot. Soon there was a whole group of us who tailgated next to each other and saved spaces for each other. Making new friends and meeting so many Browns fans was the best part of it for me.

At first, I partied right along with everyone else, enjoying the adult beverages. I was just having fun and still had no idea what was starting to unfold. After one of those first games I was walking back from the stadium with a herd of fans, not paying much attention to my surroundings, and suddenly my beehive wig was knocked from my head by a tree limb. Immediately two little kids behind me screamed, and my buddies cracked up. "Those kids are gonna be in therapy for years!" They just stood there laughing while I pleaded with them to pick up my hair and put it back on my head! At that moment I began to realize there was a responsibility that went along with being a visible fan, especially when little kids are around. The Bone Lady would have to stop partaking in alcoholic beverages on game day.

During the week, I worked at my decorative painting business. Columbus had been booming, so I was quite busy. I was a regular at the local paint store and was always striking up conversation with the guys who worked there and the contractors buying their supplies. (I think you can tell by now that I'm not shy.) I got to know the regulars, and most of our conversations were about football, especially the Buckeyes. One of the guys, knowing of my Bone Lady character and my car, told me that at every Buckeye home game he worked parking cars at the Horseshoe, the stadium where the Buckeyes play. One of the cars he always parked belonged to Lou "The Toe" Groza and his wife. If you're a Browns fan, you already know about the legendary Hall of Famer, the former Browns kicker and tackle. If not, you need to. Anyway, the painter/parking guy (I'm sorry not to remember his name) said I should come down early on a game-day morning with my Bonemobile, dressed as the Bone Lady, and he would park me next to the stadium where I could meet Lou Groza.

As with most opportunities that now seemed to be constantly presenting themselves, I jumped at the chance even though I had no idea what to expect. That game was Ohio State's homecoming, and I was one of the first to arrive that morning. I parked right next to the stadium entrance and put on my Bone Lady garb. I was hanging out, meeting some nice people, when these two guys from Sports Radio 1460 in Columbus came by and interviewed me. After we were finished, they invited me to go into the stadium with them. I went, not knowing what was to happen, and soon found myself on the field before the game, where I got to get a photo of me standing right at midfield and got to sit on the Buckeyes' bench!

When I finally returned to the parking lot, Lou Groza and his wife, Jackie, had just pulled up. I showed him my car, which made him laugh, and we took a photo standing in front of it.

He and Jackie were both so nice and I was thrilled to meet this football legend.

I thought the day couldn't get any better, but it did. A gentleman who was in his fiftieth year as an usher at the Horseshoe asked me if I wanted to go to the game. "Yes!" I said. He took me into the stadium, and we sat in the box belonging to the Galbreaths, a well-known Columbus family. During a halftime ceremony, the team retired number 45, which was worn by two-time Heisman Trophy winner Archie Griffin. What I would have missed had I not dressed up in my Bone Lady outfit and driven my Bonemobile to the stadium that day! That was such an empowering moment for me—when I realized what I would've missed if I had worried what other people would think of a woman dressed in an orange beehive showing up at a Buckeye game.

Someone told the Columbus media about my car, and Dom Tiberi of WBNS Channel 10 came to the house to interview me. I took him for a ride in the Bonemobile. He sat in the back while the cameraman sat next to me in the passenger seat. Dom was so full of energy, and he laughed during the whole ride! After my story aired that night, he called and asked if I would be willing to bring my car into the studio after the Browns' first win for *Wall to Wall Sports*, a show that aired after the news on Sunday nights. Of course I agreed, thinking it might be fun. Kirk Herbstreit was the host. I listened to him every day on sports radio and was a big fan, so the opportunity to meet him and show him my car was exciting. The first game the Browns won was against the New Orleans Saints, with a Hail Mary pass from Tim Couch to Kevin Johnson. And it was an away game, so I watched it at home in Columbus. As soon as my excitement over the win subsided, though, reality hit me.

"Oh no!" I thought. "Now I have to go do that TV show!"

Fear seeped in like a colorless, tasteless poison, turning my enthusiasm into total panic. I thought, "What am I gonna do? I can't do this! I'm not prepared. I don't know anything. Who do I think I am that I'd be qualified to go on a sports show?"

Anxiety and self-doubt engulfed me, and I almost called the station to tell them I couldn't make it. My dear designer friend Don called while I was in the midst of my panic, and I told him about it. He gave me the best advice ever, which I still use to this day. He said to just think about every question that they could possibly ask, and have my answer ready. He also told me to visualize the whole TV show experience. I had done that before with my painting projects, so it made sense to apply it now. Don and I were used to helping each other along our paths. He's always been a teacher to me over many years because every book and seminar he ever suggested changed my life in a profound way. So I always listened to him. This time was no different, and I followed his advice.

The station wanted me to bring a few fans with me, so I called my friend Jim Madden, who was the president of the Mansfield Browns Backers. He agreed, and I met him and a few others at the station. I pulled my car in the studio, and because I had listened to Don's advice and was prepared for anything, my nerves subsided. The whole experience was fun! Kirk was awesome, and cracked up seeing my car. I also met Andy Baskin, who worked at the station and now is a sportscaster in Cleveland. He's one of the nicest guys in sports, and a few weeks later, when I asked him to come to Mansfield for our Browns Backers Christmas Party for kids, he graciously agreed and said he was honored that we even asked!

I had met Jim Madden in the Muni lot while tailgating before a preseason game that returning season. He was living in Mansfield and had just become the president of the Browns Backers club there. The day he walked up to me and introduced himself, I had no idea that I was meeting not only a best friend but my true Angel on Earth. He had heard that I lived in Columbus, and he asked me if I would be interested in leading their three buses up from Mansfield for their club's home game of choice. I was flattered to be asked, and said yes immediately. On the day of that game, very early in the morning, I left Columbus in the dark and headed north towards Mansfield. Jim said he wanted to ride with me as I led the bus parade. To this day, he swears he took his life in his hands riding in my car! Like everyone who sits in the passenger seat, looking over the pile of paraphernalia on the dashboard, he asked, "How do you see?" And like always, I replied, "People see *me* and get out of my way!"

As we got to know one another during that fateful ride, I knew we would be great friends. If you were to ask him today what he thought of our first meeting, his reply would be, "I thought she was f---ing nuts!" Ah yes, my kind of friend! Jim has a kind and caring heart with a witty, outgoing personality. He has many stories from his life experiences and from with his dealings with many Browns and Indians players over the years. His business, National Pastime, arranged player appearances at various venues, and that first season he included me. So I started appearing at Browns Backers events, player signings, parades, and whatever event Jim would think up in his head. It was all new to me and so much fun! We've been unconditional friends ever since that first meeting in the Muni lot, and he has been my consistent confidant—there for me during the saddest times in my life and the best ones. If you have a friend like that, you are truly blessed.

*   *   *

The Browns won just two games in 1999. But we had a blast anyway! That first season was full of excitement, with so many Browns-related events and activities. One was a Christmas

Parade that the City of Cleveland organized to kick off the holiday season. My friend Jim thought the Mansfield Browns Backers should participate and wondered how I'd feel about leading our group with the Bonemobile. I thought it sounded like fun, and soon my creative ideas were flowing. I decided that the Bone Lady should play Santa Claus and ride on the hood of my car. I made a chair with a tall back in the shape of a bone and covered it in Browns fabric with orange fabric balls lining the edge. I attached letters spelling out "Bone Throne" on the back.

Jim always was full of ideas, too, and he suggested that Browns Backers club members act as reindeer. So thirty "Reindeer Dawgs," dressed in Browns t-shirts with antlers on their heads and dog noses on their faces, pretended to pull me and my Bone-sleigh-chariot while I sat perched on my throne, holding the reins in one hand and a whip in the other. On top of the eight-foot-long, white plastic bone on top of the car, I placed a fake, white, four-foot-tall Christmas tree decorated with brown and orange ornaments.

Tom, my sister, her husband, and their kids all participated, too. Tom drove the Bonemobile sleigh, with my brother-in-law riding next to him. We were quite a spectacle as we paraded down the street towards Public Square.

One minor detail hadn't occurred to us: with me on the hood, Tom couldn't see anything as he drove! So he and my brother-in-law were like a tag team driving crew, with Tom steering the wheel and working the pedal and the brake while my brother-in-law stuck his head out the passenger window to give directions. It was hilarious, but I wasn't laughing—I had my own issues: I didn't feel very stable sitting on my Bone perch and thought I would fall off the car, becoming Bone Lady road kill! No catastrophe occurred, however, and we won Best of Show! How appropriate for a bunch of Dawgs!

That night Tom and I headed back to Columbus, where we did it all over again by participating in the Gahanna Christmas parade. Yes, as my friend Jim said, I must've been f---ing nuts!

*   *   *

A final exclamation point for the Browns' return and the Bone Lady's first season was a trip to the Super Bowl. No, you didn't miss the Browns finally playing in the big game (hopefully that happens before I leave the Earth!). The Browns didn't make the trip—but the Bone Lady and well-known Browns Super Fan Big Dawg did!

For the season's last home game, I was out in the Muni lot tailgating with my buddies when Big Dawg came out to the lot. He was with a couple of people representing Jose Cuervo tequila who were looking for the most outrageous fan to join Big Dawg on a trip to Atlanta for a week before the Super Bowl—and then attend it! A few of my buddies were also in the running, but I was the chosen one. I couldn't believe it! I did feel bad for the others because they probably deserved to go more than I did. So before we left, I symbolically took them with me by having their pictures made into buttons that I then pinned onto my wig.

In Atlanta, there were two fans each from five different teams. It was fun to meet and hang out with them for a week. We were to travel around the city and encourage fans to do outrageous things to win tickets to the game. The only drawback was the weather—cold, with ice storms. Many of the activities were outside, so it wasn't as enjoyable as it might have been. We did, though, get to soak in the atmosphere that the Super Bowl brings.

The night before the game, I went out with a couple of the other fans: Spiking Viking from Minnesota, who sported a purple and gold Mohawk, painted face, and Viking garb, and the Titletown Clown from Green Bay, who wore a green and yellow Bozo wig and Packers-colored clown attire. The bar scene was really happening in Buckhead, a suburb of Atlanta, so we headed there dressed in all of our garb. We'd had so much fun being dressed up all week that not dressing as our characters seemed boring. Of course, with the Rams and Titans playing in the Super Bowl there were tons of fans from both those teams out in Buckhead that night. It was quite a festive atmosphere as the night progressed, until the bars began closing and everyone poured out into the street looking for a cab home. There were lots of limos picking up players, and young women were getting in and out of them. The area quickly seemed to turn seedy. We had trouble getting a cab, and I started to feel very uncomfortable. While waiting for a cab I decided to huddle in the doorway of a storefront to keep warm. Spiking swung his plastic sword while Titletown kept an eye out for an empty cab.

All of a sudden, two guys walked towards me into the vestibule where I was waiting. They said something to me in Spanish that I didn't understand and I had a bad feeling as they got closer, forcing me to back up into the doorway. My two fan compadres were paying no attention and then one guy went to reach in his pants like he had a knife or a gun. I screamed, pushing the one guy out of my way, and took off running—the best I could in my Bone Lady platform shoes! My buddies immediately snapped out of their goofing-off mode and followed me down the street. When they caught up with me I started yelling at them to get us a cab because I didn't want to die in Buckhead that night dressed as the Bone Lady! We eventually made it back to the hotel in the wee hours of the morning and I climbed into a warm bed, feeling very lucky to finally be there. The next night, after the Super Bowl, two people were killed in Buckhead (the incident involving Baltimore linebacker Ray Lewis), and after my scary experience there it didn't surprise me.

It was exciting to be at the Super Bowl, but as I walked around observing all of the festivities I noticed that there was a definite line of demarcation between the haves and have-nots. The regular fans seemed to be left out of a lot of the parties and activities. It was a very exclusive atmosphere with lots of corporate sponsors who seemed to be there to do business, and it wasn't so much about the game.

On our way into the dome, Big Dawg and I were constantly stopped for photographs. I understood why they wanted a photo with him, because he was so well known, but I was surprised that they wanted photos with me—especially since these weren't even Browns fans. I even missed the whole pregame show because so many people wanted photos. That was a moment when I realized that there was something about the Bone Lady character that people were attracted to, and it wasn't just about football. Back then, I couldn't quite figure it out because I was just at the beginning of my journey. Later on I would find the deeper meaning beneath the beehive.

Bone Lady's Tips for Fans, Part 1

BE AN EMPOWERED FAN

Life is about change. Nothing stays the same. The more you embrace that change and learn to move through it the happier your life will be. If you're an older NFL football fan you know how much the game has changed over the years. Just as the world used to be different and much simpler, the game was too. Now everything moves at such a fast pace with knowledge at our fingertips (literally), information and news obtained in an instant and a global economy.

The business of football is huge! When we now talk about players we don't just discuss their stats, the position they play, their size, their ability. We now include in the discussion the details of their contracts, who their agents are, and how much money they're making. For the majority of fans who live a modest life it is hard to comprehend the salaries these players now make. That "have and have not" reality contributes to a disconnect between the fans and the team. Some of these salaries can be so out of whack with the "real world" that I think it leaves fans not very sympathetic when a player or coach is having difficulties on the field. Years ago many NFL players had second jobs as they couldn't make a living from football. Once the games started to be played on TV, the business of football changed and grew to where it is today.

Well, fans can change with the times, too. Instead of just willfully shelling out our hard-earned money to watch and root for the team we love, we can take back some of their power by deciding how we want to participate and to what degree. Remember: you are not a fan victim! It can be frustrating to be emotionally invested with your team *and* spend lots of money to watch them only to be disappointed with their play year after year. Now we all know it's much easier to give them your money when they are winning, but as we know too well here in Cleveland that's not going to happen every year . . . if at all!

You can be a fan and love your team but you can decide to what degree you want to participate. Some fans go to the tailgate party then to the game while others choose to stay at home with their family in the comfort of their home. *No matter how you choose to watch the game, everyone is still a fan!*

BEST FOOTBALL BUDDY . . . EVERYONE NEEDS ONE!

Who's your BFB? My brother is mine. We text back and forth during the game and whenever there is any news about our Brownies. It gives us a chance to vent and to laugh! My brother is hilarious. When the game is teetering on pathetic, he will always have a funny line that will crack me up and snap me back to reality.

Also your BFB can be your contact throughout the week, and after the game they are someone to break it down with. Sometimes the day after a horrible game my brother would call, and we'd both say "I need more time. Can't do it!" When we would finally get in the mood to talk about it, we would discuss all the plays then the shoulda, coulda, woulda's. After a few hours of bitching (when the game was *so* bad) we would be able to continue on with our day. Once we had purged the previous game, then we would start to discuss the upcoming one.

You don't have to go through the fan experience alone. Your BFB is kind of like what a sponsor is to AA. They can be there to listen, hold your hand, and give you that tough love when you need it. I don't think I would be the fan I am without my BFB. He also taught me to throw a spiral with a football when we were little, and I've used those skills many times in the Muni lot (sometimes while wearing my evening gloves). HA!

BEING A FAN ON A BUDGET

Being a fan can be expensive. Here are a few ways to stretch your fan dollars:

- ***Think long and hard before buying a specific player's jersey.*** Especially here in Cleveland! If your team is constantly turning over its player roster year after year, buying new jerseys can get very expensive. You could keep wearing the jersey of a player that was on your team for a brief moment and then was gone, but that's kind of sad. Hey Browns fans— would you still sport a Jeff Garcia Browns jersey? I'd rather wear a Jerry Garcia jersey. HA! (Young kids won't get that joke!) So my recommendation is that you buy a jersey and put YOUR name on it. That way you can wear it for years as long as you still fit into it. Or when it's time you can pass it down to your kids or someone else with your same last name. Buy a throwback player jersey—those never go out of style and you are honoring that player and his legacy by doing so. Now if I'm too late giving you these suggestions and you've already spent money years ago on a player jersey and can't afford a new one, then do what many Browns fans have done . . . invest in a roll of duct tape! Put it over the old name that shares the same number and write the new name on the tape. One of the best ones I've seen was a Tim Couch number 2 jersey that said Couch on the back. The fan put duct tape before the name "couch" and wrote the words "sittin on the" . . . COUCH. HA! Browns fans are very creative.

- **Save money by NOT buying a ticket to the game**. Of course this is a personal choice and trust me I'm so glad that I went to all of those games for all of those years. I loved the experience, but now as I look back, there were some seasons when the caliber of play on the field was so bad that I had wished I had saved some of my money. Watching bad football while lying on your couch at home is a lot less painful. And when the game is over, you still have your money in your pocket!

- If you go to the game, try to **save money on parking** by sharing a ride. Everyone can chip in, plus it's more fun with more people. Or take public transportation—even more savings, and even more people.

- **Tailgate before and after the game.** Concessions inside the stadium add up fast. If you can fill up beforehand and make it through the game without leaving all of your money there, you're doing good!

- *Throwback gear is timeless.* Think about that when purchasing t-shirts, sweatshirts, caps, and hats. Check out independent retailers, where you can find some cool team merchandise for a lot less. Also, look on the Internet.

HOW TO WATCH A GAME AND HAVE YOUR TV SURVIVE THE DAY WITHOUT YOU THROWING SOMETHING AT IT

Now, if you're going to the game, well, they have security so you can't throw anything. And if those four-letter words get out of hand, they'll ask you to tone it down. But when you watch the game at home there is no security, so you are on your own. Here are a few ways to help you curb your game-watching frustration.

- *Get yourself a BFB . . . Best Football Buddy!* Every fan needs one. Mine is my brother Doe Dave. While lying on my couch watching the game, he's in his house watching on his own couch. We constantly text back and forth. It seems to relieve some frustration when you can pick up your phone to text instead of throwing the remote! As an example, this past season while watching a particular Browns QB's painful play I got a text from my brother that read, "I just want to hit myself in the head with a hammer!" I immediately burst out laughing and was able to control my arm from throwing action. We now call this frustration "The Weeden Effect." Oops—I guess I gave his name away. Hey Brandon, wish you the best with your new team. I just couldn't watch you in a Browns uniform any longer.

- *If the game gets too stressful* or the play is too unbearable to watch, I suggest you find another activity to do simultaneously. I've been known to turn on the radio and listen to the game. Actually I even do that while watching it on TV. Usually

I'm not a big fan of the national announcers who are chosen to do Browns games, so I turn on the Browns Radio Network and listen to Jim Donovan and Doug Dieken. They're great! Those two call it like they see it. They could have a stand-up comedy act if they chose to. I've also been known to scrub my toilet or clean out the sinks and bathtub while listening to the game. Maybe all that scrubbing helps me work off my frustration. And it leaves my house sparkling clean!

- *Keep your TV remote in hand* so you can flip over to a good game of football if things get too bad or if you just can't watch bad football any longer. Sometimes you need a new perspective to see what good football looks like. Otherwise you start to think that your team played well when clearly they did not (hence, delusion will set in).

- *If you are of age, you can always drink.* But for some of us others, I'll do some deep breathing exercises and will usually meditate before or after. Try it. You'll be calm and the game won't seem so horrible. And you don't get a hangover by meditating.

- *Find a postgame radio host you can relate to.* Mine is Greg Brinda from ESPN Cleveland WKNR. Listening to him after the game is like therapy for me. He lives in the now and tells it like it is. No illusions, delusions, or drunk callers (he hangs up on them!). He'll tell you what REALLY happened and not what the team wants you to "think" happened. There's no "They played their guts out" kind of talk. Also, Greg will help you decipher the coaches' press conference—whether the coach is speaking the same language or describing the game in a language that leaves you wondering if they were even AT the game you watched! Greg gives you the true perspective. Hopefully you have a favorite radio host/therapist as I do.

A Wonderful Life

Mom had been diagnosed with colon cancer, and little did I know that the year 2000 would be her last one on Earth. My sister, brother, and I became a united front of support for mom as she went through this, along with her sisters. We did whatever we could to help her during her battle, but always this deep, dark cloud of emotion hung over our heads. The one thing that got us through was the fact that we have a great sense of humor in our family. When the doctor said to my mom, "Well, if it wasn't for that cancer, you're perfectly healthy," it made us laugh, and we quoted that line all the time because it was so absurd. Damn, that cancer is such a bitch. Life can be funny in a strange kind of way, but the ride that cancer takes you on is so bizarre that all you can do is laugh at it even when you want to cry.

I would drive up from Columbus whenever Mom would need me, or just to visit. Before Browns home games, I stayed at her house whenever I could. It was hard to go on with my life. There was a part of me that felt like stopping everything and just spending all of my time with her because I didn't know how much time she might have left. Mom wanted all of us to just go on with our lives, but balancing work, family, and life's responsibilities was difficult. Cancer throws it all out of whack, leaving you exhausted.

I remember sitting in her living room on Saturday evenings before games, trying to get her mind off of the fact that she wasn't feeling well by telling her of my adventures, hoping to get a laugh or a smile out of her. My brother was the one who could make her laugh the most, but I did my best. Usually I had my glue gun out and was crafting some sort of addition to my Bone Lady outfit. She always wanted me to go to the game, and when I felt bad about leaving her she would insist, saying "Go, and I'll look for you on TV." Mom was a Cleveland sports fan too, so watching a Browns game was routine on a Sunday.

That year now seems foggy to me. The cancer haze certainly hung over me as I did Bone Lady stuff, worked and traveled for my painting business, did things with Tom, worked on our house, and helped my aunt with antique shows as we filled in for mom. It was hard for her to continue her antique business, but she needed the income, so we helped as best we could. Her home, which she'd bought after selling the house in Bath after divorcing my dad (more on him later), was an outlet for her creatively. She had transformed the house, laying wide plank floors, wooden shutters, adding an early architectural mantel and doors, and letting me paint a mural along with a floor. Customers of hers, fellow antique dealers and friends, were always stopping by, and mom would hold court, sharing her knowledge and love for early antiques. To this day, when I run into some of those people they still talk about those visits with my mom, telling me how kind and gracious she was. So when her cancer battle took a turn for the worse, I realized there was one blessing that comes out of having a terminal illness, and that is that you get time to tell people what they mean to you and to find out how much you mean to them. I told mom, "You're just like George Bailey from that movie *It's a Wonderful Life*, where he got to see what life would be like if he never existed. You get the gift of people telling you how much you are loved and how much you touched their lives."

The last time I saw my mom was in a hospice facility, where the staff were managing her transition. She never said she was going to die; as a matter of fact, no one ever said those words. It wasn't until two weeks before her passing that anyone told us she was even close to the end of her journey. This facility let you take dogs in to visit, so of course I took Molly. Mom loved Molly, and seeing her was comforting. Molly had a calming aura about her, and because she loved people she was like medicine for your heart. I was sitting next to Mom's bed holding her hand while she lay there, awake but not saying a whole lot. I was full of all of these emotions and thoughts about what my mom meant to me and how much I loved her. I wanted to share them with her, but since she never spoke of dying and was uncomfortable with the topic, I sat there not saying anything. Then this voice in my head said, "Say it!" I still hesitated, but this voice urging me to tell her how I felt about her was relentless.

So, with both of my hands lovingly clasping hers, while sitting close to her in a chair by her bed, tears welled up in my eyes as I told her she was the best mom ever and I was grateful that she was my mom and I wouldn't have wanted anyone else to be. I thanked her for everything that she'd ever done for me and for setting me on my path as an artist. By this time, tears were streaming down my face and hers as she quietly mouthed the words "Thank you." Then she asked me if I could see the people standing around her bed. I smiled, knowing who they were, and said, "Oh Mom, those are your guardian angels. They're here for you as you go on your journey. You're not alone, and everyone you've ever loved that has crossed over is waiting for you. When you see the light it's okay to go, and don't worry about us because we'll be fine."

A look of reassurance came over her face, and as I told her I loved her, a feeling of peace came over me because I had said everything that I needed to say. It seemed like I was the one sent to comfort her before her transition. I was always the one in our family who wasn't afraid of talking about my feelings or discussing my spiritual beliefs. That visit was the last time I saw my mom. I went home to Columbus, and she passed a few days later. That was how my mom was—she wouldn't leave the Earth while we were there in the room because she would think that would be painful for us, so she headed toward the light in her own private way.

Someone once told me that when a loved one passes, you need to look for the gifts, and I now know that to be true. One week after mom's passing, I received a FedEx letter telling me that I had been selected to be honored at The Pro Football Hall of Fame in The Visa Hall of Fans exhibit as the 2000/2001 fan of the year for the Cleveland Browns. So, during the last home game of the 2000 season, on a very cold, blizzardy day, I was honored on the field with a plaque. Many fans had left the stadium by then because of the weather, but that didn't matter to me because I knew mom was standing right there. As they handed me the plaque I said, "Thanks, Mom."

Little did I know how that moment would change the whole path the Bone Lady would take.

*   *   *

Within two months of Mom's passing, I jumped off a cliff and changed my life. Her death was like some sort of blaring wake-up call for me to get on my life's journey. I left my Tom, who is one of my favorite people on the planet, left my house, which I loved, and moved into a cute little house in German Village in Columbus that I referred to as the "healing house."

Leaving my life with Tom really had nothing to do with Tom at all; it had everything to do with me. Without getting into all of the details, the bottom line was our relationship had served its purpose and it was time for me to venture out on my own. Not all relationships are meant to be forever, and as the years went on the dynamic of how we related started to change. I really think I grew up during my years with him, and as I started to really come into my own, I knew deep down that I had to go on my journey alone. It was like I had grown wings and now was ready to fly out of the nest. Tom is one of the kindest, most generous people, with an infectious, gregarious personality. I met him while doing antique shows with my mom because he also is in the business. So during my years with him I learned a lot about all kinds of art: folk art, Native American textiles, and many other types of objects. Tom has a great eye and has been successful with his business as we would travel the country, antique-picking or doing shows. Plus we laughed a lot and always had a good time. But I think we both knew on some level that there was a piece missing in our relationship. It was not an overnight decision but one that was fermenting under the surface for a while. I am happy to report that he is now married, and I am and always will be grateful for the time we spent together.

I moved into the "healing house" with my dog Molly and Olive the cat. After working at my painting business during the day, I would be on the phone every night with my friend Jim, who really helped me during that time, especially while my grief was at its peak. I would drive up to Cleveland for every home game, staying at my sister's house, and also traveled around Ohio as requested for appearances as the Bone Lady. Many times I would be all "boned up," driving my Bonemobile on my way to some event, when suddenly my grief would rise up and punch me in my heart, and out of nowhere I'd sob like a baby. The flood of tears left my heavy Bone Lady makeup a pathetic mess. I'd call Jim and say, "I can't go be the Bone Lady today because I'm so sad!" He would patiently listen as my grief poured out and then he'd calmly urge me to go. "You need to go and be the Bone Lady because afterwards you will feel so much better. I promise."

Jim was right. After taking a lot of pictures with people and making them smile, I did feel a lot better. It seemed that giving of myself as the Bone Lady was like medicine for my own soul. For a very long time, most of my fellow Browns fans had no idea that I was in major grief mode. I kept putting on that orange beehive and being the friendly, smiling Bone Lady out in the world, even though underneath I was weeping. Who knows, maybe that act was the thing that kept me going.

*   *   *

In August 2001, during Hall of Fame weekend in Canton, I was officially honored at the Pro Football Hall of Fame in the Visa Hall of Fans exhibit as the Cleveland Browns fan of the year. This was the most humbling honor I've ever received. In the back of my mind, I thought, "Why am *I* being honored?" I didn't have an answer, but it felt like a current was rushing by, catching me up in the flow, and all I could do was to just go with it.

Every year, fans who had been honored would get together for a reunion. A few fans from the initial class decided to organize it. Monte "Arrowman" Short was the facilitator, and he was also the president of the newly formed fan organization named Pro Football's Ultimate Fan Association, or PFUFA for short. Not only did those fans want to get together every year during HOF weekend, they also realized that they could do some good in the world. So their mission was to promote sportsmanship and support charitable activities.

When I arrived at the hotel where all of us fans would be staying during the HOF festivities I was greeted by a few fans who were in my same class. This was the first time for all of us, and it was cool to meet some of the legendary fans from all over the NFL you've often see on TV, like Barrel Man from the Broncos, the Hogettes from Washington, D.C., Da Pope from the Saints, the Chiefs' Arrowman, the Packalope, and, of course, Big Dawg. I remember sitting in the lobby with Big Nasty from the Tampa Bay Buccaneers, who was also new to this, and we just looked around in amazement, not believing that this was even happening to us. As we shared stories, we became fast friends. During our ceremony inside the HOF, Big Nasty said, "Not everyone can play the game of football, but everyone can be a fan." That is so true, and as I got talking with other football fans, I realized there was a strong connection that bonded many of us. We had similar experiences even though our teams and our cities were different. Hearing their stories was the best part of the whole reunion because I now had a tribe of people who understood what this superfan ride was like and could share what was happening to me.

During that weekend our group was in the HOF parade, and then we went to the player induction ceremony held in the front yard of the Hall. I remember walking into the ceremony with Da Pope and Packalope, and as we passed the row of media they stopped us and took so many pictures as if we were celebrities walking the red carpet. It was a bizarre feeling. The next morning, we were honored inside the HOF with our names on a plaque along with our picture in the Hall of Fans exhibit. I felt so honored, as did the other fans who were with me.

The whole experience of my first HOF weekend event and fan reunion gave me a purpose and sense of responsibility; I felt like I was representing not only my fellow Browns fans but women who love the game. For the NFL to honor women (although not many) at the Pro Football Hall of Fame was a big deal. I could feel the historic magnitude of the honor while realizing how important the responsibility was to represent female football fans everywhere in the best light, and I decided to take that very seriously.

After that reunion, Monte/Arrowman, our president and reunion founder, called me to see if I'd like to be involved in helping put on a kids' event during our reunion. Since Canton is just down the road from Cleveland and many of the other Ultimate Fans are far away, I agreed to help. He said to me in his Southern drawl, "Bone Lady, go find some kids." Well, you would think that would be an easy thing to do but it took many phone calls and conversations before I was introduced via the United Way of Canton to the J. Babe Stearn Center, a boys' and girls' club in downtown Canton.

At the next HOF reunion, PFUFA put on a free tailgate party for kids. Each fan brought things to give away to the kids, played flag football along with other games, did face painting, had hot dogs, candy, and pop, and many of the fans cooked their typical tailgate food from their part of the country. The kids had a ball! After we cleaned up the event, Dave and Tim, who run the center, said to me that when I came to meet them to discuss having an event with the kids, they had no idea what to expect from a group of football fans but they agreed because they liked my enthusiasm and trusted that it would work out okay. Afterwards they admitted that they were impressed by how wonderful, kind, responsible, and fun all of the fans were.

Of course they wanted us back the next year because we had started something magical for the kids to enjoy. Every year the event grew as more kids and their families heard about it and PFUFA, and it continues to be a highlight of HOF weekend for the kids and their families, and also for the fans. Many kids came back every year and built relationships with certain fans.

In the big business of pro football, players and coaches usually aren't very accessible, but Ultimate Fans are—and a kid can meet them, get a picture, and have a more personal connection with the team they love.

My life changed in such a dramatic way the year after mom passed away. I will always think that she helped to facilitate my HOF honor, and as the opportunities for the Bone Lady started to multiply, I could feel her hand in that, too. Yeah, cancer sucks, and losing someone you love dearly isn't easy, but there are blessings that come out of tragic moments. I miss her every single day, but there have been so many things that I wouldn't have learned about life and myself without experiencing her death. Although I know she's just over there on the other side, I miss her here on the physical plane, and there are many times that I'd love to give her a big hug and sit in her uncomfortable gray linen chairs and have one of our long conversations. Those chairs now are in my living room, and when I really miss her, I will sit in one and feel her sitting in the other. I tell her what's happening in my life and what I miss most about her. And I know she's listening because at that moment I can feel my heart swell.

What the Hell Is an Itinerant Limner?

My art career started in a bathroom. Don't laugh, but yes, a bathroom. I hadn't ever really painted before—well, except when I was a senior in high school and did an oil painting of a cat at Mom's request. There is a very famous folk art painting of "Smut the cat," a large, charming orange tabby in a seated position that takes up the whole canvas. It just makes you smile, and Mom loved it. My attempt at recreating that folk art cat was the very first oil painting I had ever done. It came easily, and I had such fun painting it and making my Mom happy. Doesn't every kid want to make their parents happy?

I just ate up the positive validation when she framed the painting and hung it up in the house. Now, you have to understand that my mom was very particular about her house. She'd been collecting early 18th- and 19th-century country painted furniture and accessories since the 1960s, and she was a purist when it came to decorating. We basically lived in a museum. The house was built in 1830, and when you walked in the door you were taken back to that era like you had just time-traveled there. So for her to hang my painting among all of her real antiques was a big deal. It made me feel like maybe I was good at this.

I wasn't able to take art in school. I was in the band, and in junior high and high school you couldn't take both. I was good at playing the flute, was student director of the band in ninth grade, and won a musician of the year award, so I just followed the path that I was good at because I kept receiving accolades for it. I never considered that I could even be an artist, because you had to pick one elective or the other. That now seems stupid to me, since they made me take algebra, which to this day I don't understand. Guess it never occurred to anyone that maybe someone who was gifted in music might be good at art? What a concept! I did go to college—well, for one semester. That I'll explain later.

A few years later, my aunt and my cousin opened a restaurant in Brunswick, which was an addition to the meat market my uncle had owned for years. Mom was helping her decorate it because she wanted it to have a primitive country feel, and that was my mom's expertise. They had to have the restrooms done to specific building code, which left them looking like huge, plain white, sterile rooms, not at all in keeping with the restaurant's ambiance. For some reason my mom said to my aunt, "Have Debby paint a mural." Why she recommended me I still to this day have no idea, except that maybe it was some sort of divine intervention, because it came out of the clear blue.

At the time, I had been doing some freelance wallpapering and regular room painting but nothing like artwork or a mural. I'd had my own little business for about a year after learning house restoration from a real estate agent in Akron. She was renovating houses in the Highland Square area, and I had started working with her after quitting a two-year job selling Clinique cosmetics at a department store by telling the rigid HR woman to "f--- off" after she had put me on probation for not wearing my hair up and not wearing that stupid white lab coat. Within a week, I was working restoring houses.

It came as a shock to my boyfriend at the time. When he met me, I was getting dressed up every day for work with perfect hair and makeup, smelling good and looking pretty. Then, a week after quitting, I'm dressed in ripped dirty jeans, an old sweatshirt with a do-rag on my head, big work gloves on my hands, my face covered by a mask for blowing insulation into attic rafters! Poor guy, he didn't know what hit him! But I loved it and felt like I had found the real me. I loved the freedom of working for myself, and later on all of the house restoration techniques I learned would serve as the best training for the art journey I was about to embark upon.

So, back to my aunt's restaurant. After agreeing to paint the mural, I found myself in the women's bathroom, sitting on a bench staring at a blank white wall. I remember saying to myself, "OK, now what?" I recalled that the same phrase had come out of my mouth about a year earlier when I had bid a job to wallpaper a car dealership that had two-story-high walls and was by far the biggest square-footage job I'd ever bid. After getting that job, I found myself standing in the middle of the dealership trying to figure out where to begin. Some people would describe taking on jobs that you've never done before as "stepping out of your comfort zone," but at those moments I would've called it "stupid" because I was scared to death. The negative talk started to creep into my brain asking, "Why are you doing this? You can't possibly pull this off." But at that car dealership, I had no choice but to persevere because I wasn't going to admit that I was afraid, and heaven forbid I'd have to tell people I gave up. No way! So I pushed through, determined not to let the client see me sweat. I knew one thing though, and that was that no matter what it took, I would make the client happy, even if it was at my own expense. Now, sitting on that bench in the bathroom of my aunt's restaurant, faced with a new challenge, the answer came: "Go to the library."

My aunt, my mom, and I decided that a farm scene would be the appropriate subject matter since this was an addition to the meat market. At the library, I started looking through books about folk art painting to come up with inspiration. As I was poring through the shelves of art books, one flew off the shelf and landed on the floor with its pages open. I looked down, and there was a large photograph of a nineteenth-century landscape mural at Winterthur Museum in Delaware. I took one look and I knew in that very instant that this was what I was going to do. Not what I was going to paint for my aunt's mural, but what I was going to do for a career. It was as if my destiny had just fallen on the floor and opened up in front of me.

My first day on the mural job, while driving from Akron to Brunswick, I passed an old run-down farm that had a great red barn with a sewer-tiled silo. That would be my pattern for the farm, and once I got started the rest seemed to flow like I wasn't even having to think about it. Even I was amazed as I worked my brush in short, rhythmic strokes to emulate long grass in the wind. I don't know how I knew how to do that, but it felt like some other force was orchestrating the whole process and I was there just to physically carry out the task.

When I was finished, my mural was a hit. My aunt loved it, saying she'd had no idea I could do that. Yeah, I didn't know either! I got lots of great feedback, and soon she had me paint the men's room, which was an even bigger hit. The townscape of row houses I painted, with a cobblestone street, was nice, but the rear end of Daisy the cow that I put directly over the urinal, with her head turned looking back at the user, sparked the most conversation and got quite a few laughs!

A few months later, Mom suggested that I paint a naive landscape mural on a huge roll of paper that she could hang in the back of her booth at antique shows. She had a show coming up in Sheffield, Massachusetts. So I painted the backdrop, hung it up in her booth, and got my first painting client. Well, first one that I wasn't related to. A couple from the upper West Side in New York City had just purchased a country house in Stockbridge, Massachusetts. He was an accomplished documentary filmmaker and she was a successful author. They invited me to come live with them for a month while I painted their dining room, compensating me with a minimal fee and promising to take me around the Berkshires and to New York, where they would introduce me to a very famous trompe l'oeil artist. They knew I was just beginning my career because I didn't have a portfolio to show them, but they were supportive of my learning as I went along. Now, you may be thinking it was strange that I would even consider living with people I had just met. But in my gut it felt right, and the style of painting I was doing had a tradition of painters living with their clients while they painted for them.

In the late eighteenth and early nineteenth century, wallpaper was very much in fashion, but it was very expensive and only wealthier people had it in their homes. I don't know exactly who was the first painter to see an opportunity to provide the same look to those people who didn't possess the funds to buy wallpaper. A few itinerant painters (artists who traveled) worked throughout New England, painting people's walls for room and board. Landscapes were a popular subject. Some of those itinerant painters started to gain a following by word of mouth or ads in the local paper. One of the most famous was Rufus Porter. He wrote a book in 1825, *A Select Collection of Valuable and Curious Arts, and Interesting Experiments*, in which he gave step-by-step instructions. He was also an accomplished inventor and founded *Scientific American* magazine. Many of his murals still exist, as do murals by other painters who had followed Porter's instructions and painted in his style. My new Stockbridge clients liked that I was researching the history of that style and seemed excited that I would be painting their dining room walls in that tradition.

But instead of using the word "painter," I called myself a "limner," which is what some portrait artists of the time called themselves. Limners took likenesses of people when composing a portrait, and I felt like I was taking likenesses of the landscapes I was painting. Limner derives from the Latin *illuminare*, which means "to light up," and that felt right to me because when you are doing what you are meant to do while you are here on Earth, you shine your own unique light.

I packed up my little Mazda hatchback and drove to Stockbridge that summer. There I stayed, living in my clients' country house, enjoying my time with them and painting their walls. I followed the *Curious Arts* book, but since it was written in 1825, I had to substitute some of the materials that Rufus Porter used with modern-day ones. I could actually feel him there with me as I painted. At one point, I was struggling with getting the background to look the way I wanted and kept repainting the same wall over and over. After about the fourth time I had painted it, I went to paint it over again and dipped my brush in the gesso to cover it up. As I went to put it on the wall, my brush flew out of my hand as if someone had grabbed it and thrown it across the room! Startled, I stopped for a moment, then went and picked up my brush, chuckling at the thought that Rufus, my teacher from the other side, had had enough of my do-overs and just wanted me to move on already!

Over the month that I was there, living as a twentieth-century itinerant painter, I adapted well to the lifestyle and got to experience what it was like to live in the area. I was teaching myself how to paint a mural while on the job and was enjoying everything I was being exposed to. A whole new world was opening up, and I was a passenger along for the ride, sucking up this new adventure the way you drink the end of a milkshake through a straw and you keep sucking it in even after it's gone. Towards the end of my painting journey with these particular clients, they took me to New York for a couple of days, as promised. They lived in a posh Upper West Side apartment by Central Park. At their urging, a friend of theirs, who was a world-renowned trompe l'oeil artist, agreed to meet with me at his studio to see my work and offer me some guidance.

I had no portfolio, just a few Polaroids of my bathroom art and that huge rolled-up mural on paper that I had hung in my mom's antique show booth a few months earlier. The day of my meeting, I headed out to get a cab, not realizing that my eight-foot-long, rolled-up mural wasn't going to fit in the backseat or the trunk. It was a beautiful morning, so I thought I would just enjoy the New York City streets by walking to this man's studio. With a tote bag slung over one shoulder containing photos of my bathroom murals and my mural tube propped up on my other, I proceeded to walk down the street. I thought this would be a short walk, but as I passed block after block after block my shoulders were getting really tired, and soon I figured out that this was quite a hike—about fifty blocks later! Exhausted, I arrived at the artist's studio—an elaborate place with every surface of walls, woodwork, and furniture painted in some sort of faux finish. It was intimidating, and I thought to myself, "What am I doing here?" Obviously without any real painting experience or training under my belt, this was a definite "cart before the horse" moment. I felt like I had back at that car dealership, when I had to just push through my fear. That cliché "fake it 'til you make it" was never so true—it kept showing up in these unsure moments of my life. I learned to just hold my head up high and pretend I belonged.

The famous artist I came to see certainly didn't put me at ease. He was kind of arrogant and really couldn't be bothered with me. Here I was in what seemed like a palace full of faux marble and murals; I felt so out of my league. Now I laugh when I think of carrying that eight-foot-long mural fifty blocks through New York and showing him my bathroom mural Polaroid pictures and then unrolling this large paper mural right in the middle of his grand trompe l'oeil palace foyer as if he were the emperor and I the court jester! Guess I really do have balls! He didn't give me much feedback, let alone any real encouragement, and instead pawned me off on his worker-bee artists in the back room.

They took me to lunch and shared with me the real workings of the famous artist's studio. It seemed he designed the painting but they executed it and did all of the work! On the outside, he was the all-powerful Oz and they collectively were the man behind the curtain. All of them were artists in their own right, many with an art school background. They came to New York to live their dreams but found themselves working for this guy in order to pay their bills. I could tell that most of them didn't enjoy their job at all. Listening to their stories of how difficult this guy was to work for and how they longed to spend most of their time creating their own art made me sad. The longer they stayed there, the days, months, and years passed, with them getting caught in life's current, and soon their dreams of being their own artist were getting smaller and smaller like a ship moving toward the horizon. I came away with a newfound clarity: I wasn't going to end up like them. As I walked those fifty blocks back, retracing my steps to my clients' flat, I realized that I had to go my own way—even if I didn't know the direction.

My Stockbridge experience was finished, and I returned home to Akron. Soon, my art career was building momentum without my even trying. I was getting jobs strictly by word of mouth, and my work was published in several national magazines. A mural I painted in my mother's house was photographed for *Early American Life* magazine. I went to Hartford, Connecticut, to paint for another client, and that job ended up in *Colonial Homes*. I continued to travel, living with my clients while I painted.

I was asked to demonstrate my mural painting at an antique show in Newburyport, Massachusetts, which led to painting a flower shop called Twigs on Bleeker Street in New York. The owner put me up at the infamous Chelsea hotel. Many rock stars over the years have stayed there. It's probably best known as the place where punk rocker Sid Vicious allegedly killed his girlfriend. The hotel certainly wasn't glamorous, but I was excited about being in New York. While sitting at the desk in my room, watching a cockroach scurry up the wall, I had to remind myself, *But this is a famous hotel!* Hey, I got to live the life of a working artist in New York City, and I'm sure most of them had run into a cockroach at some point in their career! Paul, who owned the flower shop, had just done a magazine shoot and had tons of gardenias left over, so he gave me two garbage bags full of those sweet smelling blossoms and told me to put them in the bathtub in my room. Oh, the place smelled like heaven! I just had to keep my eyes closed and forget about the cockroach and the run-down interior.

That mural ended up in *House Beautiful* and *Colonial Homes* magazines, and when the flower shop moved to a different location, the restaurant that took over the space kept my painting. That was much-needed validation for a self-taught newbie to the art world. It made me feel good.

The other huge job I did early on in my career was for Ralph Lauren. I knew a guy from the antiques business who sold a lot of furnishings and accessories to Ralph, and when they were looking for someone to paint an early-nineteenth-century mural, he recommended me. I stayed with friends in Greenwich Village while I went to Seventh Avenue for one day and painted a mural over a fireplace in the women's wear showroom. It was bizarre because I got off the elevator in this high rise and walked right into what looked like an early log cabin. A gentleman dressed in old jeans and a Navajo sweater greeted me, then took me to the area where I was to paint, saying to me, "We like what you do, so just do it." Then he walked away, leaving me alone to create. I never forgot how they just let me do my thing. I figured that must be one of the reasons the Ralph Lauren company has been so successful: hire the right people and let them do what they do best. Micromanaging an artist is never a good thing, because when you try to control the outcome of a piece of art, it turns out contrived, never reaching the potential of what it could be. Wow—there are many other areas of our lives that we could apply that way of thinking to!

In the 1990s, people around the country were hearing of me and my painting talent. I'm sure the magazine articles helped get the word out, but most potential clients were finding me by word of mouth. I didn't advertise, but the right people seemed to show up at the right time. One of them was my soon-to-be dear designer friend Don. The Newburyport antique show at which I painted had led me to him. His former college roommate was at that show and picked up my brochure. At the same time, a friend of his who was in the floral business had seen the flower shop in New York and told him of me. So out of the blue, I got a phone call from Don one very snowy Ohio day. We immediately hit it off, talking for a long time; it was like talking to an old friend.

Even though it was snowing a lot, I suggested we meet the next day, and I drove up to his studio in Cleveland. The feeling I had when I met him was one of such familiarity. He told me about a house he was working on in Kentucky and said they were looking for someone to paint a mural. I left that meeting knowing we would be lifelong friends (and that client in Kentucky also became a great friend and client for many years). I learned to follow Don's guidance, and one of his biggest life-changing recommendations was for me to attend a painting workshop in Florence, Italy.

The workshop was so expensive, but Don said to me, "You can't afford not to go." Boy, was he right—that workshop opened so many doors for me. I met other decorative painters, gained access to new products and techniques, and secured future collaborations on jobs that never would have happened without my going on that trip. Plus, just being in Italy changed my perspective on how life can be lived! There I was, surrounded by great art and architecture, eating delicious food, drinking local wine, walking a beautiful Tuscan countryside, and spending time having a huge meal with family and friends right smack in the middle of a work day. The Italians know how to live!

Traveling all over the U.S., along with my growing business in Columbus, kept me very busy. I was not only painting, I was getting opportunities to design a few clients' homes. Here, again, were more cart-before-the-horse moments when I didn't let fear rush in and get the best of me. As the years went on, I stayed on my painting path, acquiring new clients with new projects, working with certain designers who kept feeding me work. Of course I was and still am grateful that people would pay me to paint for them, but as the years pass and you gain experience under your belt, you reach a turning point.

What I enjoyed about being a freelance artist is that the work is often different from project to project. It's not like a structured job that has milestones or measuring points where you know you're moving up the ladder. So I was just out doing my thing, and I wasn't stopping to reflect on my progress or map the road I wanted to take with my painting career. Until one day, when I hit a definite turning point. Usually, I didn't turn down jobs, even small ones. What if there wasn't a next job? I wasn't even sure I had a choice to say "no" to jobs. But one day that changed.

A very nice lady asked me to paint pink bows on a piece of furniture for her. I am going to be vague about the details because I wouldn't want to hurt this woman's feelings. I went to her house and it wasn't horrible, but it was so overdone and over the top that it looked like a hundred flamboyant decorators had simultaneously thrown up in there. Get the picture? In fact, saying it was overdone is an understatement. When she showed me the piece of furniture I was to paint, I looked around the room, which was like a kaleidoscope of color, pattern, fabric, wallpaper, and knickknacks, and I thought, *Of course you want pink bows on this piece of furniture!* Being the client-pleaser that I was, I became a little painting trooper and painted the best damn pink bows that I could!

She was thrilled, and wrote me a check as I packed up my stuff as fast as I could. I just wanted to forget my contribution to that designer travesty! If you've ever had a one-night stand and done the notorious walk of shame, well, that's what it felt like walking out to my car. After loading up my supplies I got in the driver's seat, looked at myself in the rearview mirror, and thought, *You are nothing more than an artist hooker! You just went and prostituted yourself for money!* My perspective about my art career changed that day. I realized I *could* say no to jobs that didn't fit my career path or just weren't experiences that I wanted to have. And as I started to practice that concept, it turned out that the painting work didn't end when I turned down jobs. Selectiveness strengthened my integrity, and I felt very good about that.

Years later, during my Bone Lady ride, I would encounter a similar situation, not with painting but with being able to say no to people who wanted me to appear at their events. Again, it took me a while to be able to turn people down, but when I did, I realized that setting boundaries with other people is taking really good care of yourself.

*   *   *

When people who know me as Debra the artist find out that I am also the Bone Lady, they usually want to know if those two worlds ever cross paths. On occasion they do. I have done paintings and decorative painting in a couple of players' homes. Once, while still living in Columbus, I had to go see a client out in New Albany, an upscale area of brick Georgian homes and architecture that Les Wexner, the founder of The Limited brand, created years ago. He bought up all of the farmland in that northeastern suburb of Columbus and created a sort of village environment where many of the executives who worked for his companies could live. For us in the painting and decorating business, it was a boom time, and the building seemed to be never ending. Since the communities are planned, the building and landscape codes are very strict. So one day while heading out to see my client who lived in one of those huge Georgian homes, I had to drive my Bonemobile because my other car was in the shop. I pulled up in front of this beautiful brick home in my orange, Browns-helmet-painted Volvo wagon with the huge white bone on top and, needless to say, I attracted a bit of attention. My client came out with an inquisitive look on her face. While I was getting my supplies out of the car I said, "Oh don't worry, I'm not going to paint your house brown and orange!" She laughed! So my two worlds do cross even though it's a rare occasion.

I had a strange occurrence while at a Browns' event, a party unveiling new uniforms. I was doing my Bone Lady thing, meeting fans and taking pictures, when this guy and his wife came up to me and introduced themselves. Years earlier, they had bought my mom's house, where I had painted one of my very first murals. The previous owner after my mom kept it, and so did they. I had received a few Facebook messages from them over the years because somehow they knew that the Bone Lady had painted the mural. Right after we said our goodbyes, I walked about two feet away and a younger gal came up to me, telling me that her mother had bought my friend's condo, where I had painted a mural in the sunroom years earlier. Now that was a little bizarre, to have two people, back-to-back, approach me about my painting while I'm at a Browns event dressed as the Bone Lady.

Those two worlds are no longer separate but are both a continuing part of my life. When synchronistic events like that happen, it feels like a little nudge from the universe that I am indeed on the right path.

TALES FROM THE BONEMOBILE

BONELESS

After one of the many home losses against our bitter rivals—*ugh*—the Steelers, when we got blown out again, my friend Tracy and I packed up the Bonemobile to head home. We got on the Shoreway heading back towards Lakewood and all of a sudden I heard this *swooosh*, followed by *bam*! The car immediately felt different, and in a panicked voice I said, "Oh my God I think the bone fell off the car!" Sitting next to me in the passenger seat, Tracy burst out laughing, and she continued to laugh hysterically with tears streaming down her face.

At the time I didn't think it was funny. First, I didn't know if it had hit anyone and, second, I was emotionally attached to my bone! (Okay, that's funny.) I yelled to Tracy to stick her head out the window and look to see if it had indeed fallen off. She rolled down the window and stretched herself out, looking up at the roof of the car. Then she looked at me and nodded her head "yes," while still laughing uncontrollably.

I had traveled all over Ohio, through wind, thunderstorms, and snowstorms and I'd never had a problem, then after a loss to the Steelers there it went, flying off my car like some bad karma that was being fulfilled. I thought, *Of course it flew off after a loss to the Steelers!* The next game I pulled into the Muni lot "boneless" and it just didn't feel the same! Mike Siedel from the Weather Channel, who always had me on when he reported from the

Muni lot, did most of his live shots that day about the fact that I no longer had a bone on my car. Two fellow Browns fans and die-hard Muni lot tailgaters, Scott and Bruce, offered to make me a new bone for free! I will never forget their generosity, and that gesture reinforced what I already knew about Clevelanders: most of them are always willing to help someone out.

KEYLESS

I took a friend to a game, and upon leaving the stadium I noticed that my car key was missing. I had always kept it in the pocket of my Bone Lady hoop skirt but this time it was nowhere to be found. I took a cab home to get my other car and possibly find a spare key. There was no extra Bonemobile key to be found so I got my other car and picked up my brother to head back to the Muni lot to meet a locksmith there.

We pulled into the Muni lot after most of the fans had left and it looked like one of those war-torn cities you see pictures of on the news. We had at least a two-hour wait because the locksmith was totally confused as to where we were. He thought I had said Detroit not Muni lot and he had a hard time understanding English, so after we hung up the phone I just hoped that he was going to show up. As my brother and I sat there we watched these giant alien-like truck sweepers suck up all of the trash left lying in the lot by fans. The wind was blowing and the trash blew all over like tumbleweeds in a deserted ghost town. It felt like we were in some *Twilight Zone* story where we were the only ones left on the planet. Or a *Seinfeld* episode.

The locksmith kept calling for directions. He was totally lost. Every time he called I tried to enunciate clearly, and I even and tried spelling, "Municipal parking lot! Cleveland, Ohio! Not Detroit!" My brother and I just looked at each other and laughed. Finally the locksmith showed up in a brand new luxury car,

leaving me to conclude that the lock business must be pretty good. Within two minutes after getting out of his car he had the Bonemobile's driver's door open and told me it would be $100. So I got out of the car and, while facing the Bonemobile, I proceeded to count out exactly all the money that was in my wallet—and that was $100. Then he told me that he can't make me a new key but if I have the car towed he would come to my house the next day and for $300 would make me a new key.

While he was telling me this I noticed something stuck under the driver's side windshield wiper. And there it was—my key! Are you kidding me? If only I had found that earlier I would've still had $100 dollars in my wallet. But I was relieved that I wouldn't have to have it towed and spend another $300 to get a new key made!

Hanging out with my brother was the best part of that evening and to this day we still talk about it and laugh! The next game, while tailgating, a guy came up to me and asked if I had found my key under the wiper. I said yes and was curious how he knew it was mine. He replied, "Bone Lady, you have the only Volvo in the whole parking lot!"

CLUELESS

Yes, I have been stopped by the cops in the Bonemobile. Once. I was still living in Columbus and had gone to a charity event the night before. Early the next morning, while driving my car back to the storage shed where I kept it, I got pulled over. The cop walked up and he was not very nice—actually he kind of yelled at me. "Do you know this whole car's a violation! How can you see out of this car, the windows are blocked? Oh and that *thing* on the top, is that secure?" I replied, "Oh, you mean the bone?" I was thinking of also telling him what I usually say when people ask how I drive that car: "I don't have to see, because people see me and get out of my way." But I decided that wouldn't be a good idea because he'd probably think I was a smartass.

Then I thought, Really I just did a charity event last night and he's harassing me? So I decided to use my cute Bone Lady charm to try and connect with him. I asked if he was a Browns fan, thinking if he was he'd go easy on me. Immediately he barked out a firm, "No!" With a quirky smile on my face I asked, "You're not a Steelers fan, are you?" "No, a Bears fan!" That was the end of me being cute as he proceeded to write me an $80 ticket for obstruction of view. I wanted to argue my case because my car wasn't any different than those that people fill up when they're moving—except of course mine had a huge bone on top and was designed to attract attention. I've always wondered since then, though, if my car had been a "Bearsmobile," would I have gotten that ticket?

Where's a Phone Booth When You Need One?

Now that we carry phones around in our pockets or on our wrists, the phone booth is long gone. What's a superhero to do? Or a superfan? Just like Clark Kent transforming into Superman in a phone booth, I've had to change into my Bone Lady garb, or out of it, in all kinds of places. I'm not fighting crime, so my need wasn't quite as urgent as Superman's, but I have had to "Bone up" while out in public, in parking lots, the backs of cabs, the side of the road, in vans and cars, in back alleys, and on city sidewalks.

In 2002, the NFL decided to hold a huge party in Times Square for the kickoff to the football season. Visa, which was still sponsoring its fan exhibit at the Pro Football Hall of Fame, contacted me and asked if I would be willing to go to New York City with a few of my fellow HOF fans to do media for them to promote their fan exhibit. I was so excited to be asked and immediately said yes.

Before the trip, they had a couple of us do some radio interviews. So one day, while working at a painting gig in Columbus, I had to call in to a New York radio station along with Mickey T. "Boss" Hogette of the infamous Hogettes from Washington,

D.C. First the radio host talked with Mickey T., and then it was my turn. I was supposed to talk about the Visa Hall of Fans program and what it was like to be a fan honored in the exhibit. Well, I never got to talk about anything because the radio host, in his thick New York accent, just wanted to talk about what Art Modell had done to Cleveland and Browns fans. Right when I had a chance to speak, the host cut me off and the interview was over. It happened so fast, and it left me feeling frustrated and disappointed that I couldn't get the message out. I apologized to the marketing people and vowed to myself to never let that happen again. From that day on, I learned to be assertive and to turn the interview around by getting my message across immediately instead of waiting for the host to ask. Boy, have I used that tactic a lot! Funny, but it seems like many radio and TV hosts like to hear themselves talk, so why even have a guest?

During the trip to New York, we spent the whole day doing media, and since I was the only female fan on the trip, as usual, they wanted me to meet the editors of *Sports Illustrated for Women* (which is now defunct). Decked out in my Bone Lady garb, I went up to their offices, which were in some high-rise in the city, accompanied by a marketing person. We had a really nice visit, and they talked about how they'd love to do a story. As we were leaving, I noticed the entrance to *Sports Illustrated* was right across the hall. At first I thought I would come back another time to get a photo of me in front of their offices. But then my gut told me to take the photo right away, because I might never get the chance again. So I seized the moment and snapped that picture. And now, whenever a similar experience occurs that might be a once-in-a-lifetime moment, I don't take it for granted. By the way, to this day I've not made it back to the *Sports Illustrated* offices, but I do have that photo of me that I took on the last day I was there.

Towards the end of that afternoon, the NFL Kickoff in

Times Square was about to begin. There were crowd barriers lining both sides of the street with a gauntlet of media platforms down the middle and a huge stage at the end. The Visa marketing people were taking us through that media gauntlet, lining up interviews. The one they really wanted to get us onto was the CNN platform, but they were having difficulty making that happen. We were hanging around in the space between the crowd barriers and the platforms when all of a sudden they yelled, "Bone Lady, we want you and Birdman to go up onto the CNN platform now!" They wanted us live on the air, immediately, so we climbed up onto the platform while I was assuring the marketing people that this time I would be getting their message out, no matter what. My friend Birdman from Philly decided he would just do his usual squawk and leave all the talking to me. So we were up high on this platform, looking down at this never-ending sea of thousands of people lining the street, waiting for the interview. It was our turn, and the CNN reporter got one line out introducing us and then I took control by quickly commenting that the NFL Kickoff felt like a national holiday. I got out the Visa Hall of Fans message, I smiled, then thanked the reporter and Birdman finished it up with his trademark squawk! Whew! It went quickly, and I don't think the reporter knew what hit him!

After we climbed off the platform, the marketing people were all smiles, congratulating us because that was the one interview they wanted. As we walked down the street in that empty space between the crowd and the media, people were snapping photos left and right. Enrique Iglesias was playing live on the stage singing his hit, "Hero," and I thought about my mom, and I had a feeling that this role of the Bone Lady was truly meant to be.

Eventually we made our way to Planet Hollywood, where the NFL was having its party. I could only stay for a bit because I had to catch a plane home, and it was too bad, because the party was pretty cool. I hailed a cab and in the back seat got dressed in my normal Debra clothes. I started to laugh as I was taking off my shirt, watching the driver's eyes in the mirror staring at me in the backseat. I told him, "Go ahead and look because you're going to anyway, so enjoy the view!" I don't think he understood me, but I could see him smile.

The next night I had to go to a Browns Alumni event in the Flats in Cleveland. When Bernie Kosar arrived, he came up to me and said, "Bone Lady, I missed you last night at Planet Hollywood. Birdman said you had just left!" I love when unexpected things happen so easily without any effort at all, as if those moments were meant to be part of the course of your life.

After my mom passed, I vowed I would find a way to communicate with her on the other side. One of my clients/friends who regularly went to see the Columbus-based psychic Bill Mitchell urged me to go. The first time I met him the first words out of his mouth were, "Your mom got you to come here, not whoever told you about me." Over the next few years Bill would play a huge role in helping me hone my own intuitive gifts and supporting me on my Bone Lady path. Many times I would visit him, upset over some guy I was dating, and he would give me insightful information, although usually not what I wanted to hear at the time, and it would get me back on track. Every time I would see him for a reading he would tell me, "Always be the Bone Lady, no matter what." Bill helped guide me in my decision to move back to Cleveland and to trust my gut if it was right for me to move.

His advice underscored the fact that I was spending most of my time working and had no social life except for Bone Lady appearances and going to the games. My breakup with Tom had been amicable but most of our friends had chosen sides, staying friends with him and not me. Certainly that didn't feel good, but I figured it was time to move on from my past. So with the help from my niece and her friend, we packed up my house into a huge truck and, with my dog Molly and Olive my cat, we headed north for the next chapter of my life.

*   *   *

Shortly after my move to Lakewood, Ohio, I got a call from CBS Sports saying that they wanted Big Dawg and me to do a commercial for the kickoff to the 2003 NFL season. They flew us to New York for a couple of days. We stayed in Times Square and then shot the commercial out in a suburb. The commercial was cute because I got to stand on the porch as the Bone Lady and yell at Big Dawg for being a "bad dog" for attacking the mailman! We had such a good time with the crew and the producer/director Shaun Robbins, who down the road would reappear during my Bone Lady ride. You never know when you meet people what kind of a part they may play in your life, even if it's a small role.

When the commercial aired, it was around Hall of Fame weekend and our PFUFA reunion. Our local CBS station, Channel 19, knew of the national commercial and sent this very nice, pretty blond-haired reporter named Denise to interview me at the reunion. She started to ask me the same questions I'd been asked five hundred times before on our local stations, so I stopped her mid-sentence with, "Why don't we talk about what is going on now with the Bone Lady?" She was a little startled, but sort of laughed. Then we talked about the stuff I wanted to talk about, and she let me put some Bone Lady paraphernalia on her, like my glasses and a feather boa, and we took a photo sitting on the hood of my car. I said to her, "You're nothing like the typical blond news chick! You're fun!" She asked me where I lived, and I told her I had recently moved from Columbus to Lakewood. Then she suggested that I meet some of her girlfriends because they, too, were all single, and they were always going out and doing things. That was the beginning of a dear sister-like friendship with Denise. She became a conduit, leading me to a group of women friends who to this day mean so much to me and who I will know for the rest of my life.

I quickly settled in my new life in Lakewood, meeting new painting clients, commuting back to Columbus for other painting jobs, and going to games, Browns events, charity functions, and even getting to do some freelance TV work for Channel 19. Good thing I was settled in: the next season brought so many opportunities for the Bone Lady that they came rushing in like a swift, raging river.

*   *   *

I met Tom Megalis, a morning DJ on WMMS radio, while tailgating in the Muni lot. He had a camera in his hand and asked if he could shoot a quick little film of me in full Bone Lady regalia, with my car, for their website. I said "sure," and he was so funny that we hit it off immediately. Then he wondered if I'd be interested in coming in to do football picks on their radio show. Of course that answer also was a "Yes!" Browns radio announcer Doug Dieken would call in to the show, and we would all give our predictions for every game that NFL Sunday. We had a blast, and I really liked being on the radio. That gig went on for a couple of years.

Tom Megalis is a very creative person with a resume full of his own animation, acting, commercials, visual artistry, comedy, and film. We found ourselves working on a documentary about the Bone Lady. He would follow me around with his camera and get footage of me in action during that whole season. It seemed like the right time back then, but now I know it was too soon to make a film about the Bone Lady. More in my life had to unfold.

At the Hall of Fame weekend that August, I walked into the lobby of the hotel where we were having our PFUFA reunion, dressed in my Bone Lady garb and carrying my beehive wig in my arms. Arrowman from the Chiefs and I had just come from the Hall of Fame, where there was a ceremony for the new class of fan honorees. At the front desk stood these two scruffy-looking guys dressed in t-shirts and jeans. One guy proceeded to ask me if that was my car outside, referring to the Bonemobile, and of course I answered him in a smart-ass kind of way—"Uh, yeah, how could you tell it was mine?"—while waving my hand down the side of my outfit. With this very strong nasal New York accent, he told me they were with HBO's *Inside The NFL* and they were looking for the Ultimate NFL Fans who were in the HOF. At first I thought they were full of you-know-what because what they were saying and how they looked didn't match up. Also, it was late morning on a Monday and we were far from the HOF, so I never expected national media to be in our hotel lobby. But I talked with them anyway, and soon they revealed their identities. One was the comedian Jim Florentine, who I had heard of from a show on Comedy Central called *Crank Yankers*. The other guy was Donny, his sidekick and partner in crime. They wanted to interview me in front of my car and also a few of the other fans. Then we shot a skit and when we were finished, I offered to drive them back to the Hall of Fame in the Bonemobile. They jumped at the chance, and with Jim in the backseat and Donnie with his camera in front with me, we headed off on our afternoon adventure.

First we went through the drive-through of a fast food restaurant, and while Donnie was shooting, Jim fed me lines. We laughed as the poor kid who waited on us didn't know what hit him! I wish I could remember all of the one-liners that went back and forth. I wonder if they still have that footage. We then arrived at the HOF for the game, and they continued to get more footage for the show. When it aired on *Inside the NFL* it was hilarious! I loved it!

What started out as a tiring morning and an early trip back to the hotel turned out to be one of the best, most unexpected fun days ever, and if I hadn't talked with those two guys because of how they were dressed, I would have missed out. Over the years, I've learned that many people who work in creative fields like TV, film, and radio don't dress up because they want to be comfortable. I get that; if you ever saw what I wear when I paint, well, let's just say it's not pretty!

A similar situation happened while I was still living in Columbus, going into my second season as the Bone Lady. The Browns played a scrimmage near our house at Columbus Crew Stadium against the Indianapolis Colts. After it was over, I was walking out to the parking lot when a man who wanted to meet me stopped us, explaining that he was the general manager of the Crew soccer team. I told him I only lived two miles from the stadium and he said, "Bone Lady, we have to get you here for a game." I explained that soccer wasn't my thing but I would try to attend if I could. At that moment, another older gentleman walked up. He was very unassuming, dressed in a ball cap and tan khakis. We continued to shoot the breeze for a few minutes longer. I looked at the lanyard around the neck of the man wearing the ball cap. His name tag read Lamar Hunt. It wasn't resonating with me even though I was staring at his name, and it didn't dawn on me until he walked away that he was actually *the* Lamar Hunt, owner of the Columbus Crew and the Kansas City Chiefs, and also the man who actually coined the term "Super Bowl!" Wow! The joke was on me because he was such an unassuming man, dressed in his ball cap and Dockers, that I never thought that was him! Later when I shared the story with

1. When the Browns returned in 1999, I woke up one morning convinced I needed to paint my Volvo wagon like a Browns helmet and install an eight-foot-long bone on its roof. My Bone Lady outfit soon followed. This photo marks the beginning of my strange journey in a beehive.

2. While painting my mother's casket, I had the Browns game on the radio. When the game got exciting, the funeral director popped in and asked me to stop yelling—there was a service going on next door! He wasn't too happy, but Mom would have understood.

3. The "Itinerant Limner" at work. Here, I'm painting a mural in a home in Lebanon, Ohio. My art career may have started in a bathroom, but it's taken me to some interesting places!

4. Sunday dinners at Grandma and Grandpa Darnall's left an imprint on me. This small table commemorating those meals is a piece I did for an exhibit of self-taught artists at the Wexner Center for the Arts in Columbus. The painting is of 94-year-old Grandpa in his garden with his dog, Jim; I painted it on the day of his funeral. He led a simple life but was the richest man I've ever known.

5. It was a cold, snowy final game of the 2000 season at Cleveland Browns Stadium—so cold that most fans had left by the third quarter. But I was thrilled to be on the field to receive a plaque honoring me as Cleveland Browns fan of the year and recognizing my selection for the Visa Hall of Fans exhibit at the Pro Football Hall of Fame in Canton.

6. I'll always partake in some spontaneous dancing when given the chance. For most of my life, I wasn't comfortable being the real me. But when I put on a costume I discovered there's a certain freedom when you're not dressed as yourself. As I became more confident from all the public appearances, I realized that the Bone Lady and Debra were really the same person, no matter what outfit I wore.

7. Homecoming at the Horseshoe in Columbus, 1999. I met Lou "The Toe" Groza and had the best day ever! None of it would've happened if I hadn't "Boned up" first.

8. "Myyy friend" Jim Madden sitting in the Dawg Pound with me for a game. A Browns Backers chapter president and a true angel—and just one of the many great people I've met tailgating in the Muni lot.

9. In Seattle with another woman who loves football and wears a tiara: my friend Mrs. Seahawk. We were honored the same year in the Visa Hall of Fans. Her husband, Mr. Seahawk, was honored the following year. Wish they didn't live so far away. For some reason they and other Seahawk buddies get the urge to call the Bone Lady late at night but forget the time difference—I've been awakened at 3 a.m. many times!

10. Don Cockroft is looking for a space to sign the Bonemobile. You can never have enough stuff! Every inch of the interior is covered in Browns memorabilia and Dawg Pound paraphernalia. There's even a bust of Elvis in there somewhere. (He was a Browns fan, too.)

11. Standing on the steps at the hallowed Pro Football Hall of Fame in Canton, with fellow NFL fans honored at the Visa Hall of Fans. If there really was such a thing as fashion police, we would all have been arrested! (*Joe Cahn*)

12. Holidays are just another excuse for me to get out my glue gun and decorate! The Cleveland Christmas parade was no exception. Notice the "Bone Throne" on the hood of my Bonemobile. I took my life in my hands while riding perched up there.

13. With the guys in New York City promoting the Visa Hall of Fans: Mikey T. "Boss" Hogette, Cowboy Bob, Big Nasty, Weirdwolf, True Blue, and some New York TV show host dressed in Jets gear. Yes, there are a lot of guys in the Ultimate Fan world. But don't forget the gals: almost half of all NFL fans are women!

14. At the big 2002 NFL season kickoff event in Times Square, in front of thousands of people. Here, I'm on the CNN perch with Birdman from Philly. I talked, he squawked! The TV interviewer didn't know what hit him.

15. You never know the effect you have on others. When a kid wants to dress up like you, well, that's the best feeling ever! Michele from Crestline was my "Mini Me." I told her if she wanted to dress up again I'd take her to a game with me—and she did!

16. How many people have a photo of the day when they met a dear friend for the first time? I knew Denise and I would be friends when she let me dress her in some of my Bone Lady garb.

Arrowman from the Chiefs and his wife Stacy, they told me that Hunt would come out and tailgate with them in the parking lot at Arrowhead all the time and that they'd gotten to know him over the years and found out how down to earth he was. I learned not to let a ball cap and khakis ever fool me again!

*   *   *

Back to that 2004 season of wild Bone Lady opportunities. I and a few guy fans from the HOF were flown out to New York by Visa for the NFL kickoff. We did some local media, but it was a much different experience from the first time, and it almost felt like we were being auditioned for some other gig. Actually, we were, because a few weeks later into that season the same group of guy fans and I were flown out to Los Angeles to appear on *The Best Damn Sports Show Period* and *Jimmy Kimmel Live*. Tom Megalis went with me so he could get some film footage of my adventure in LaLa land.

We arrived, making a beeline so we could arrive in time for the Jimmy Kimmel taping. On the way, Tom sat in the front seat of the cab while Mikey T. "Boss" Hogette and I changed into our respective costumes in the back. I think that's the only time I was in the backseat of a car with a guy where we both put on dresses! Ha! Then the cab pulled up to the curb on Hollywood Boulevard, and while standing on the embedded stars on the sidewalk, I put on my hooped skirt and beehive. We were soon reunited with our fan comrades, waiting in the green room while they got our gig together, then we shot a short skit with Jimmy's cousin Sal.

The next day, after waking up early for radio interviews, we all walked over to the Fox lot to tape *The Best Damn Sports Show Period*. Fellow Clevelander Chris Rose was the host, and he was so welcoming. At one point after we were interviewed we had to partake in a tug of war with jerseys of the two teams that were playing that weekend. The Browns were playing the Raiders at home, so Spike the Ultimate Raider Fan and I had to go against one another. Chris immediately jumped in to help me out, as a fellow Clevelander would, and of course, we won! Indians pitcher Brian Anderson was on the show, too. After I got home, that Sunday while tailgating before the game, Brian showed up in the Muni lot to surprise me! That was a great moment. You just never know who you will meet and where you will meet them again!

*   *   *

I was traveling to Browns Backers events and going to the games. I even went to some away games, especially after making friends with other HOF fans from around the league. I went out to Seattle with Mr. and Mrs. Seahawk, Kiltman, and Cannonball—and had a ball! Also Arrowhead stadium with Arrowman, Tampa Bay with Big Nasty, and Lambeau Field with my buddy Packalope. All of these were awesome experiences. In turn, some fans came and sat in the Dawg Pound with me. Bearman from Chicago, Lady Titan from Tennessee, and three Hogettes—Howiette, Spiggy, and Nickette—all took some harsh abuse from a few fans in the Dawg Pound, which I found to be ridiculous because these were my friends and really good people who, although they rooted for the wrong team, didn't deserve to be treated badly. Don't get me started on that subject! While the Hogettes were here we went to the Berea Children's Home and also did a charity event to benefit the Cleveland Chamber of Commerce. The Hogettes donated their appearance fee to Coats for Kids here in Cleveland, which really left an impression on me. No matter where you go you can touch lives and make a difference.

My life seemed to be going well. I was getting some painting jobs, but most of my time was being spent as the Bone Lady. The opportunities were snowballing, and I was being swept up in it because it was fun and exciting. I felt like I was supposed to be doing everything that involved being the Bone Lady, not just because Bill Mitchell had told me to "be the Bone Lady no matter what," but because it felt like the right thing for me to be doing, even though it took my focus off of my art career. The opportunities over the years were varied and often unusual. Speaking to groups of kids at schools was and is always a highlight for me. At those appearances, as I told my story I would encourage kids to listen to their own inner voices and "be who you are," because there is no one on the Earth quite like you. Their reaction to that message was fuel for me to continue my journey, as I realized that this character was indeed touching lives in a positive way.

*   *   *

After moving up to Cleveland, I finally had a social life of my own because I had a group of girlfriends to hang out with. Occasionally I'd meet a guy I found interesting enough to date. I've never been a big dater because I don't like all of that boring blah blah small talk that most people do when you first meet them, and I'm a little on the quirky side (don't know if you noticed that about me). Deep down, though, I was really wanting to find that special guy who I could connect with and who "got" me. Always hopeful that he would appear one day, I just kept on living my life as it was unfolding and enjoying myself along the way.

But after a few years aboard the wild Bone Lady ride, the fact that I was going to most of these events and doing most of these activities by myself was getting old. In the beginning, lots of people had wanted to go with me to the games and other events. My brother, for instance, at first went to all of the games with me, but one day he just said, "Going to a game with the Bone Lady is a pain in the ass. You can't walk two feet without being stopped for a picture!" It wasn't always fun to be my sidekick. One of my friends started calling herself "Here Hold This," because that's what people would say to her when they wanted a picture with me! I was starting to notice some negative backlash that came along with the limelight. But as superheroes do, I persevered. I kept on being the Bone Lady 24/7, and stayed on my wild ride, yet I was always keeping one eye out for that nonexistent phone booth that would transform me.

Leroy Kelly and
Chicken Livers

This is a hard chapter for me to write because I'm going to talk about a very deep emotional wound that I've carried with me my entire life. Sometimes we are hurt unintentionally by someone who loves us yet doesn't even know how their behavior, or lack of it, affects us. How we interact with others can cause a rippling effect like a stone thrown in water.

My dad didn't come home a lot. When I was a kid, I just thought that's what dads did. I never questioned it or thought it was any different from any other family. He had his own business and came home a couple nights a week and on weekends. Mom pretty much took care of the house and us three kids. We were told that he would stay downtown after work to play cards and entertain clients. On the weekend, golf was his first priority, so we didn't see him much when the weather was good. That's just how it was. He was living his life and wasn't very involved in mine.

I was too young to remember living in the house I was born in, on the west side of Cleveland. When I was three, we moved out to Richfield, which back then was like moving to the country. We moved to a huge, grand, early Victorian-era house. Growing up there was like living out a childhood fantasy. The house sat on a couple of acres with a huge red barn in the back, with many trees to climb and swing on, and a pond for ice-skating and catching frogs. The tree-climbing and frog-catching weren't my thing but more my brother's. I would play along, pretending that I liked both of those activities, but I was scared to death to climb up high in a tree, and frogs were slimy and gross. I was trying to fit in, but the real me was more of a girly girl, dressed in a skirt, carrying a little patent leather purse. We have home movies of me jumping in a pile of fall leaves, holding onto that purse while I jumped.

The couple of acres that the house sat on was surrounded by woods, which we would explore for hours, picking blackberries and digging for early artifacts left by the original owners of the house. Mom started collecting antiques around the time I was born, and she had an antique shop in the upstairs of the barn. We had dogs, puppies, cats, kittens, ducks, a pony at one point, and a couple of lambs as pets.

Our childhood seemed like magic, and mom made sure that it was. She grew up during the Depression, with her mom raising her and her sisters. Their father died when she was young, and even though times were difficult, my grandmother made sure that holidays were a big deal for her girls. Mom kept that holiday legacy going, and Christmas for us was over the top. We always had a Christmas tree that touched the twelve-foot ceiling, a smaller tree in the kitchen, we made tons of Christmas cookies, and decorating the house inside and out was a major priority. This was way before Martha Stewart came on the home-keeping scene, but when she did she had nothing on my mom. As an example, mom decorated our home in the mid-1960s with candles in every window, which now you see all of the time but back then no one did.

Mom was a trailblazer and was able to carve out a life of

her own with her decorating and antiques business even though she was a stereotypical 1960s housewife. Most moms back then stayed at home to raise their kids, but her interest in antiques not only helped her to furnish our house but gave her an occupation later in her life.

By the time I was eleven, we moved to my mom's dream house in Bath, which was just down the road. She had wanted a house that was built in an earlier time than our 1867 Victorian. The new house was smaller, but the 1830 construction date was exactly what she was looking for. Instead of twelve-foot ceilings, a grand hanging staircase, and carpet throughout, this house's ceilings were much lower, more like seven feet, with hardwood floors throughout, and fewer and much smaller rooms. It had an authentic quality that felt like you were living in a museum. Mom edited all of the furnishings, getting rid of things that didn't fit in with the time period of the house. So we ended up with furniture that wasn't very comfortable and slept on rope beds. If you don't know what that means, well, let's just say ropes held up the mattress and it was like sleeping on a board. Not the most comfortable! We did, however, have a sofa, although mom would've gotten rid of it if it hadn't been for dad needing a place to lie down while watching TV on the rare occasion he was home.

When he was home, our routines changed, and everything revolved around Dad being there, like a force of nature that blew in one day and was gone the next. Everyone liked my dad. He was kind, funny, handsome; people liked to be around him, and we weren't an exception. When he was home, he became the center of attention. Dinner became a huge evening production, with him usually cooking or grilling out. He liked to cook, and would grill steaks or chicken or make one of his favorite dishes like breaded pork chops, steak Diane, fried squash, zucchini, and chicken livers. When he cooked, we didn't eat until very late because he took his time making the meal. It was like a ritual with him, first making his pitcher of martinis, then sitting down while slowly sipping them and dragging on a Camel cigarette. In between, he would go into the kitchen and complete another step in his cooking process. When his martini glass was empty, he would tell my sister to "go do your job," which meant she was to get the pitcher out of the fridge and fill up his glass. I was always envious that my sister got to do it, though once in a while he'd ask me, calling me "daughter number two."

My sister had a very special relationship with my father. She was the first child born and had five years alone with him during a time when he was much more involved with being married and having a family life. Then I came along, and ten months later my brother showed up. I'm not going to complain about being the middle child, "daughter number two," but there is some truth to birth order and not getting much time to be the baby that I'm sure was a contributing factor for some of that lacking attention. My poor mother! She must've been exhausted!

My sister got to do her job, and although it wasn't a conscious decision, I'm sure I felt like I wanted something of my own to share with my dad. I have a few memories of him attending a couple of my softball games and band concerts in junior high and high school, but pretty much it was Mom going to everything because Dad was MIA.

The nights when my dad made sautéed chicken livers, no one in the family would eat them except me. Everyone else thought they were gross and wouldn't even consider giving them a taste. He'd bread them, then sauté them in sherry and serve them on a saltine cracker. I ate them up. It became our thing, and on the nights he made them he'd say to me, "Debby, I'm making your favorite, chicken livers!" I'd smile with excitement because my dad and I had a connection, but underneath a feeling of dread would come over me that I wouldn't let anyone see. Okay, now I have to confess: I hated those gross-tasting chicken livers! Not just because I'm now a thirty-year vegetarian, but because they just tasted horrible! I pretended to like them and would cringe on the inside while I chewed and then swallowed those disgusting pieces of breaded liver on a cracker. I never told anyone I hated them, probably because it was the only thing that I shared with my dad that was just ours and I didn't want to give that up. I guess I was starving for his attention and was willing to eat whatever he served.

Wow, that's a powerful revelation that just came to me while writing this, because I could also use that line to describe some of my relationships with men. It's kind of pathetic to think I would eat something so disgusting and pretend that I liked it just so I could connect with my dad. I so wanted him to like me, spend time with me, and be interested in my life. That really has never happened, even after all of these years. Later in my life, while in therapy, I learned how important the relationship is between a daughter and her father. That relationship lays the foundation for every relationship a girl will have with the men in her life, even after she's become a woman. I don't ever remember him ever telling me I was pretty, and I certainly wasn't Daddy's little girl. Most girls want to have a special relationship with their dad, and I was no exception. I translated his lack of attention into thoughts of my not being good enough or worthwhile enough for him to be around. If only I could've been prettier, thinner, smarter, or liked things that he liked, then maybe he would've come home more often. He had no idea that I would have jumped through flaming hoops for his attention if that's what it took.

Sundays when I was a kid were the best days because the day usually was spent with family. Many Sundays we would go to my dad's parents' tiny little house in North Royalton, where all of the aunts, uncles, and cousins would gather for a huge meal. My grandma would spend hours preparing a delicious, cooked-with-love, country-style meal, most of the ingredients of which were grown by my grandpa in his garden. Being a part of a family in which the simple things in life were the most important was a great way to grow up. My grandparents didn't have a lot of money and led a very simple life, yet they were the richest people I've ever known because to me they had everything. During golf season, my dad would meet us there afterwards or not come at all. The family would always be thrilled to see him, not just because he wasn't around often but because everyone liked being around my dad.

We didn't go to our grandparents' house as much after we got older, and especially during the fall months. Since there wasn't golf then, Dad would be home. Mom would make a fire in the fireplace, and football would be on the TV. The feeling of a cozy home and all of us together gave me a sense of security that I didn't always feel, but on those days all was right with the world. Of course we watched the Browns play, but for my dad football wasn't only for pleasure—it could mean a big payoff if he picked the right team to win. Yes, he was a betting man. No one game sticks out in my memory as a particular bonding moment between my dad and me; all I know is that whatever was happening on a Sunday, the Browns game was always on in our house, like background music to our lives.

Of course, my brother was a football fan, too, taking an interest at a much younger age than I did. He knew, and still does, the names of most of the marquee players of that era, along with a lot of other Browns players. I didn't know much about football back then, but I remember picking Leroy Kelly as my favorite player. He ran the ball a lot, and because he was good it was easy to root for him. Looking back, I think I liked him because my dad did and maybe because my brother did too. I don't remember for sure if that was the reason, but sometimes at a young age kids like what their parents do. Certainly football was another connection that I was looking to have with my dad. I don't know the exact moment I became a Browns fan. Maybe it penetrated my DNA, maybe when I was born, but certainly when I was growing up, living in a home where the Browns game was always on, being a fan passed from one generation to another.

*   *   *

Well, not only did being a Browns fan stick with me for my life; so did my wound with men. It's a cliché that girls tend to fall for men like their fathers. In my mind, I would think there was no way was I going to do that, but after a lot of self-reflection and review of my relationships, that is indeed what I did. I'm not saying it was a bad thing, because I learned a lot about myself as a result (and am still learning). Isn't that the purpose of relationships anyway? Don't they serve as mirrors so we can see ourselves, our thoughts and behaviors while we interact with others?

I believe that people show up in your life when they are supposed to, and not every relationship is supposed to continue throughout your whole life. Sometimes you dance for just one song. I may have picked emotionally unavailable men, even ones with some sort of addiction issue, but I also was attracted to their other qualities, which my dad also possessed, like being kind, funny, and handsome. I used to joke, "Put me in a room with a bunch of men, and I'll be attracted to the most dysfunctional one!" That wasn't always the case, but there was some truth to it. Maybe I was comfortable with how those men treated me because that's what I knew from childhood. In any event, my relationships with men have been quite the learning journey.

Still, I'm such a romantic and I do believe in a meant-to-be kind of love. Sometimes even when I knew in my brain that a guy might not be the right choice for me, I didn't listen to that message but followed my heart anyway. Looking back, I wouldn't have changed any of those choices of men that I made, because by having those experiences, even if they ended in heartbreak, I was able to gradually heal the wound that I've carried with me my whole life. I guess I'm a work in progress, learning while I'm living.

I made a choice a long time ago to no longer eat chicken livers. I try to take better care of myself by being much more assertive and striking boundaries with men. I don't always do it perfectly, but at least I'm aware of the reasons why I make the choices that I do. As far as Leroy Kelly and picking him as my favorite player, well, that was a great choice regardless of the reason. Over the years, I've gotten to do appearances with him, which was thrilling for me, and not only was he a great player but he's also a nice person. Even though I'm much more selective with who I let into my life, I'm still out there in the dating world. I'm dating without a destination and enjoying each man who comes into my life because I believe they are supposed to be there at that moment, at least. I still have some learning to do, but over time my choices of who I do it with get better and better.

Bone Lady's Tips for Fans, Part 2

A FEW TAILGATING TIPS

Joe Cahn, America's Tailgater, has always said that "tailgating is our community social." He is so right, especially in this town. Since there are only eight home games during the regular season, everyone seems to come out to tailgate even if they aren't going to the game. Oh and if your team has been losing year after year and the actual game is not so enjoyable, then "Thank God for Tailgating!" One of the best parts is that you have all kinds of people from all walks of life, all ages, different races, economic situations coming together to partake in this game day ritual. The love of their team, city, and the game of football seems to be the common denominator that brings these diverse groups together. That's a beautiful thing that can add to the enjoyment of your game day experience. You can have a lot of fun but sometimes, with lots of alcohol consumption, it can get out of hand. If you are new to tailgating and want to know what to expect, I'm here to pass along a few tips and share a couple of stories.

Be Prepared

- **Plan ahead.** Talk with your BFB (best football buddy) and make your game day plans. Get there early to get your spot.

- **Plan who is driving home.** Don't decide that after you consume beverages; that's too late. (And remember to look out for fellow fans who have been overserved, and make sure they're safe.)

- **Prepare your vehicle** the day before by filling the tank with gas. Especially when it's cold—you might want to run the engine periodically to warm yourself up. Watch so you don't run down your battery.

- **Pack up the night before.** Decide who is responsible for bringing what.

- **Be sensible with your outfit.** (I know, one look at me and you see that I don't take my own advice!) Dress for the weather— layers when it's cold are best—and be prepared for all kinds of weather changes. Plastic ponchos that fit in your pocket for rain are great, as are hand warmers for cold weather. (Don't put a hand warmer on bare skin; it will burn.)

- **Be a good human and use common sense.** Why is it that sometimes at a tailgate, kindness and courtesy go out the window? Sure, give opposing fans some harmless ribbing— but don't cross the line into vulgar and violent. Remember: you are always representing your city and your home. Have fun but don't be a "you-know-what." A lot of people bring their families, including kids, so just be respectful.

- **Feed the cops.** That's a nice perk for those who have to patrol the lot. Over time, you'll get to know them and they you. If you're kind, they'll return the attitude.

Portajohn Survival

- FYI portajohns are the cleanest early in the morning!

- Don't wait until desperation creeps in. Always get in line before you get to that point.

- If you're in line waiting and aren't that desperate but there's someone who looks like they won't make it, be kind and let them go ahead of you. Good Karma comes back to you!

- Ladies if this is your first time using a portajohn, that pocket hanging on the side is NOT there to hold your purse. It's a urinal!

- Bring your own toilet paper and hand sanitizer. Don't rely on those items to be in the portajohn when you use it.

- Be careful where you keep your phone! Many phones have ended up IN the portajohn abyss because they fell out of a pocket. You DO NOT want to have to retrieve your phone from there. Trust me.

- Same goes for your game tickets. I suggest you wear a lanyard around your neck with a plastic pocket to hold your tickets. Use it too if your phone fits in there!

Burgers and Wings and Brats . . . Oh My!

Why does football food fare always involve eating animal flesh? Times are changing in the culinary world so it's time for some alternatives to be available. Okay, so how does a vegetarian or a vegan find something to eat at a tailgate? Well if you've been a non-meat eater as long as I have you learn to plan ahead and bring your own food. My tailgating buddies always took such good care of me as they knew I didn't cook. So make some friends, walk around the parking lot, and discover that everyone is so generous that they will feed you. If you do bring something make sure it survives the weather conditions. It's been so cold before that pickles were frozen solid! Make sure when it's hot to bring enough ice to keep your food cool enough. Also plan to have food for after the game. Instead of sitting in traffic, why not enjoy an après-game meal. You'll also save money by not eating at the stadium. This is the part where I would be listing vegetarian recipes but there's a slight problem: I don't cook.

Like a lot of veggie eaters I eat a lot of raw food. Also, I have my favorite prepared veggie salads that I buy at my local health food store. Since I live alone I can get enough just for one; otherwise I'd be wasting a lot of food.

If you are a cook and you're the one who uses your culinary skills for the tailgate, why not have a vegetarian option available? Many people don't know how to cook for veggies or vegans so why not learn more about it? What would you make? Share some of your recipes with your tailgate buddies!

Festooned, Fabulous,
and Fearless

I've been described as "festooned" on three separate occasions. Of course, I was dressed as the Bone Lady when such a description was bestowed upon me. I think festooned is a great word. It gives you the mental picture of someone being festively adorned—and the Bone Lady certainly has adorned herself, especially her hair, in quite a celebratory manner. I've had women come up to me at games or while I'm out doing an appearance dressed as the Bone Lady, and say "You're my hero! I love what you do, and I wish I had the courage to dress up like that!"

I guess I never thought of it as being courageous because I was, especially in the beginning, just doing it for fun, and fun usually doesn't involve courage. Or does it? I do think going out in public dressed in an outrageous costume does take a strong sense of self. There were many moments when I didn't feel strong in my self-worth, but I just went ahead and pushed through any fear of ridicule. My response to women who commented about me being their "hero" because I had the nerve to step out of the box was humorous: "You don't get out much, do you?" Or, "Uh oh, we're in trouble if I'm your hero!"

But in all seriousness, it may be a little messed up, but I felt a lot more comfortable being me while wearing a costume. There is a certain freedom you feel when you aren't dressed as yourself. You can be you without any sort of conforming censorship. A costume acts like a suit of armor that protects you from negative comments or any ridicule. Well, most of the time they just bounced off of me, but once in a while one would penetrate and I wouldn't feel so good.

For years, I kept the Bone Lady separate from Debra. I don't know why, exactly, except that they felt like two completely different people. I didn't like people to see the Bone Lady without all her stuff on. But over the years, I started to slowly reveal my true identity and to share Debra with my Bone Lady world. As I was feeling more confident and sure of myself, I realized that Bone Lady and Debra were really the same person, no matter what outfit I had on. At times I had no choice in keeping my anonymity because my girlfriends loved to "out" me to a group of guys when we were out on the town! Keeping the two personas completely separate didn't make sense once I realized that the Bone Lady was the real me and that true self-worth and confidence comes from inside yourself, not from what you are wearing.

For most of my life, I wasn't always comfortable being the real me. When I would let the real, unfiltered me out by acting goofy or giving a strong opinion to someone who disagreed with me, I'd feel so uncomfortable and awkward, like I had done or said something wrong, and then I waited for some sort of reprimand. The reprimand, of course, would never come, yet the excruciating feeling of vulnerability would stick with me for a very long time, like I had some secret that was naked to the world and that everyone saw. I was always like this. Growing up with a false reputation that redheads are also hotheads certainly didn't help. When I would get angry, I was told it was because

I had red hair. How ridiculous was that? I translated that my anger meant something was wrong with me.

In my early thirties, when I just wanted to feel better, circumstances led me to talking with a therapist, and I ended up seeing her for many years. It was like I went to Debra school, learning what a healthy life, family dynamic, and relationships looked like. She would refer to all of those outside sources that make you feel temporarily good—accolades, compliments, clothes—as frosting. Frosting was nice, but you needed to have the cake first. She told me that you can have cake without frosting and feel full and satisfied, but frosting without cake never fills you up. Even knowing that, it took me a long time to apply it to my life. Eventually I did, and with a lot of soul work, learning about healthy relationships and discovering who I really am, I finally was able to bake that beautiful, delicious cake. Sometimes I still like frosting, but now, for the most part, I no longer need it.

I always felt different, like a fish out of water, for most of my young life, and being born with a huge head of curly red hair didn't help. It was a blessing that I now appreciate (even though I do lighten my hair now), but when I was younger it felt like a curse. On my dad's side of the family, one person in each generation had red hair. The previous one to have it was my late uncle Pat, who I never knew because he was killed in a tank two days after the Korean War ended. His photo hung on the wall of my grandparents' house, and when they spoke of him they always talked about his red hair and the fact that I was the only other one in the family who had it. It felt special, on one hand, having red hair, but when I started my school years it became another story. It was a rarity to have, but my peers didn't celebrate it like adults did. Adults commented on how special it was; kids called you nicknames "Red" and "Carrot Top." I went along with it, but deep down I just wanted to be like everyone else. Funny how others seem to define you when you're young by something that you dislike about yourself, and you don't want that to be the definition of who you are. I so envied my sister, who had dark blond hair, and even though it was curly she would set it on huge pink rollers to make it straight. It was the 1960s and 1970s, and that California look of thin, blond, straight hair was in style. I certainly didn't fit that style, and when I looked in the mirror I hated what I saw. How ironic that now I proudly wear a huge, orange beehive wig for all the world to see.

I never felt comfortable in my own skin, particularly my body. As far as body image, well, let's just say I developed at a very early age. I remember in third grade when I was eight years old a boy came up to me at school and blurted out, "Do you know what you have that the other girls don't?" My eyes got wide while the fear of being singled out as different from the other girls welled up inside of me and I meekly asked, "What?" "Tits!" He yelled and then ran off. I was crushed, mortified! I just wanted to fit in. Plus when you're eight you just want to play baseball and kickball with the boys, not have them see you as different. When I went home and told my mom, she wasn't much comfort. In her defense, I think she was just as uncomfortable in her own body, and at that time puberty, sex, and changing bodies were not things she wanted to discuss. Heck, my older sister was the one who taught me how to shave my legs when puberty hit—at least there was someone to show me the ropes of being female!

As my breasts developed, no one paid attention. Was my mom pretending that maybe they'd just go away? No one ever thought to get me a bra. It wasn't until an older cousin came in from California for the summer a year later that I was even told I needed one. She gave me a training bra. That phrase always makes me laugh. Training? Like breasts have to go to boot camp like two good little soldiers! What are they training for, anyway? She gave me the bra while we were at a family reunion. I put it on, and then put my white crocheted top on over it. Feeling very proud, like I had just experienced a rite of passage, I went outside to play baseball with all of my other cousins and family members. My older cousin, Gary, took an immediate notice of my see-through top and quickly started calling me "D Bra." Oh, I just wanted to die of embarrassment! Instead, I laughed it off and played along with everyone's jokes. After that day, I took the bra off and didn't wear one for another couple of years! No "training" for these girls!

Through junior high and high school, I still felt inadequate. I looked around at other girls in school, and they seemed to have it all. In my eyes they were all prettier, thinner, and more popular than I was. Here I had this voluptuous body with extra weight and this hair that I hadn't made peace with. Even though adults would tell me that I was pretty and had such a pretty face, that didn't matter because I hated what I saw in the mirror. I lived in this dual world where what I was being told didn't match how I felt. I hated getting my picture taken and would just cringe seeing one of me. Even now, though I've probably taken a million photos dressed as the Bone Lady, I still have lingering feelings of that inadequacy I felt as a kid, especially when I have to take a photo as Debra. Sometimes that awkward, uncomfortable kid still shows up. Just because I'm a grown adult on the outside doesn't mean that little Debra isn't still inside. Have you ever looked back at photos of yourself from years ago and you thought you looked awful back then, only to now see how beautiful you looked? If I could've seen then what I see now life would've been a lot easier!

In junior high I wore braces for three years. It was worth the pain and hassle of having metal on my teeth all that time, but I can't say that I ever felt pretty with them on. I was friendly, outgoing, belonged to student council, played the flute in the band, was on the freshman volleyball team, and worked on the school paper. When I got to high school my sophomore year, things changed. I started to really feel uncomfortable about myself, and even my accomplishments didn't matter. The inadequacy that I felt when I compared myself to other girls in school became so painful. A lot of my friends had boyfriends, and I thought there was something wrong with me because I didn't. When they would go out on dates on the weekend, I stayed home, spending the evening in my room listening to music and dreaming of love.

By my senior year, I wasn't a happy camper at all. I can't pinpoint one specific reason, but I went from participating in everything to quitting it all and not wanting to go to school. Add to that the things going on at home involving my brother getting into trouble with drugs, my sister being away at college, my dad still not around that much, and my mom at her wits' end trying to figure out how to handle it all. I went through the motions without any real direction. It was the late 1970s, and back then there wasn't much help or support available to deal with my brother's situation. This was between the 1960s drug culture and the Nancy Reagan "Just say no" drug programs of the 1980s. The cops would bring my brother home on occasion, and as his drama grew, my problems paled in comparison. I just went on like nothing was wrong, but I was very unhappy. I could see how distraught my mom was over my brother's situation, and I felt like I had to try to help her help him.

I stayed home a lot and missed a lot of days at school, quitting most of the activities I was involved in. I remember during my junior year, the counselor, who shall remain nameless, wanted to see me in her office because my lack of attendance was a concern. After I confided to her everything that was going on at home with my family and with me, her advice was, and I quote: "Debby, did you ever think of maybe wearing a dress to school?" I thought to myself, *What? Are you kidding me? I know I wear jeans most of the time, but did you hear everything I'd just told you?*

Like my brother ran away and is living down the street from the school, doing drugs and you people aren't doing anything about it? Wow! That was a dose of reality, an example of how delusional the people in charge really were! On the outside, everything at school looked perfect, but there were many cracks, and kids were falling through them.

Here I can make my publisher happy and segue into the fact that Jeffrey Dahmer was a classmate of mine. I was reluctant to discuss this publicly because I didn't want it to be used in a sensational manner, but as long as I'm discussing the dysfunctional atmosphere that lingered among the adults in charge at our high school, it seems an appropriate context to mention him in. It didn't surprise me that Jeff slipped through the cracks with no one paying attention to his behavior, because many other kids did, too.

Bath, Ohio, was sort of like that movie *The Stepford Wives*, in which people living in an upscale community went around wearing false masks pretending that everything was wonderful and life was perfect, but that wasn't the truth of what was going on beneath the facade. There were kids with serious drug problems and other issues. Kids who were gay couldn't come out and tell people of their sexuality because the atmosphere of our culture wasn't ready to let them. It seemed like there were a lot of suicides, not only with kids but also parents in the community. In our high school, you had a separation between the jocks who were the popular ones and the "burnouts" who didn't participate in the school culture but hung out and had the reputation of being troublemakers and doing drugs. If you weren't one of the popular ones or a high achiever, it seemed like the teachers and faculty didn't want to be bothered with you, and basically you were ignored, even though behind the scenes many of the "popular" ones were also doing drugs and drinking—just without gaining the same reputation.

The high school faculty's brilliant idea for dealing with kids smoking in school was to give them a designated smoking area outside. But cigarettes weren't the only thing they were smoking, and every morning the guys dealing drugs pulled up right next to that area. There was so much going on in that school that the adults seemed to be clueless about. I don't know why they were so disengaged; all I can figure is that we were in a time that fell between generations. Our parents were used to keeping family issues secret, and to them it was important to put a game face on when out in the world.

I remember feeling so frustrated by the fact that no one was helping my brother that I ended up going in front of the school board and asking what were they doing for those kids who were involved with drugs and becoming lost. It just fell on deaf ears because, although they didn't want to admit it, they just wanted these kids to get through school so they wouldn't have to deal with them.

There were signs of Jeff Dahmer's dysfunction. Not serial-killer signs, that I knew of, but we as his classmates knew of him being drunk in class and acting goofy. I certainly wasn't a close friend, but in junior high we were in the band together and were next to each other in the yearbook.

By my senior year, I had enough credits to graduate, so the last semester I just took blow-off classes. One of those was a marriage class, and it makes me laugh because I've never gotten married! For the class, we had to pair off and pretend like we were. The football coach was our teacher, and he seemed to relish it, pairing the jocks with the cheerleaders, the popular guy with the popular girl. But when it came time to pair me up, he put me with Jeff because we were alphabetically a fit, Dahmer/Darnall. So, yes, I guess you could say that I was briefly "married" to Jeffrey Dahmer. I can joke about that now, but in actuality he was usually drunk, very quiet, and not wanting to participate. It wasn't an easy project to work on. I always felt sorry for him because he got picked on a lot. When our ten-year reunion came around, while discussing what people were doing with their lives, he was the one I wanted to make it big in life and show up all those guys who had made fun of him. The whole horrible tragic experience of what he did was not the notoriety I wanted for him. I could go on and tell you how it felt to know someone who ended up being a notorious killer, but all I will say about it in this book is that no matter how awful his actions were, I always saw him as a human being who did monstrous things, not as a monster. He was some mother's little boy, a father's son, someone's boyhood friend. It's an easy way for us to separate killers from us, calling them monsters, because if we see that they, too, are human beings, it scares the hell out of us. We can't imagine they're anything like us at all.

When I heard the news that he was killed in prison it didn't surprise me, but it saddened me. He was very intelligent, and had started to talk about his urges to kill and what those feelings were about, so maybe we missed out on learning more about what causes a human being to cross that line into becoming a killer.

*   *   *

Okay, enough of that.

After high school, I attended Bowling Green State University. I wasn't sure what I wanted to do with my life, and no one really asked. I think because my sister went there and graduated, I just followed what she did. I had no direction for my life, and I still carried all of those self-loathing issues. So what did I do when I got to college? Partied! That seemed to numb the bad feelings, and it was fun—well, at least for one semester. After that, I wasn't able to continue my education at Bowling Green. So I left and went back to my high school summer job at Hale Farm and Village, where I gave tours and worked as the candle maker. Working there was right in my wheelhouse—with my mom's interest in antiques, she had taken us there many times, since I was three years old. It felt like home for me, and I enjoyed speaking to groups of people while giving demonstrations.

That year, my brother graduated from high school and my sister moved to California and got married. Everyone was getting on with their lives. My work at the museum was seasonal, so I also got a couple of little retail jobs at the local mall. Eventually I wanted to have a "real" job, so I went to see my dad at his business, thinking that maybe there was a place for me there. He said there wasn't, and when I got home Mom kept asking me questions about the woman at the front desk. That was the beginning of the end of Mom and Dad's marriage. Apparently, that woman had been the reason, for all of those years, that my dad hadn't come home. That isn't my story to tell so I won't go into great detail except to explain how it affected me at that time. It was hard to watch my mom go through the hurt and pain that divorce brings, along with the realization that her life that she knew was changing forever. My dad went on to marry the other woman who was in his life. Not too long ago, I found out that he had met her when I was five and that they had been involved for all that time.

For the next couple of years, my life was full of chaos, not just because my parents were divorcing but because I had no direction or sense of where I was going or what I was doing. All I wanted to do was escape. I was partying, smoking pot, doing the typical drugs that everyone else was doing at that time, along with drinking and being promiscuous. I briefly moved to Florida to be with a guy, and then moved back, bringing home a different guy. It was all a haze of acting-out behavior for about two years, with no permanent relief. It was like a self-destructive illness and I couldn't find the cure.

Eventually I got a job selling cosmetics at a department store, and the guy I brought back with me from Florida returned there after realizing he wasn't a good influence on my life. I will always be grateful to him for leaving because even though it was painful, it was the moment that my life started to get better, and I started to head in a more positive direction. That didn't happen overnight, but at least it was a start.

I worked at that department store selling cosmetics full time. I started dating a guy who had moved in across the street, and soon we were living together. My life seemed to be improving, and my partying days began to wane. Sitting around the living room with friends who were always stopping by to smoke pot started to get old. They talked about all of the stuff that they were going to do, but they never seemed to get out of the chair to go do it. I started to gain interest in other things, and that's when I started to work out at the gym, became a vegetarian, and started feeling better about myself.

Over the years, people have told me I should be doing some modeling. I never took their encouragement seriously because what I saw when I looked in the mirror obviously wasn't what they were seeing. But one day, at my mom's urging, I decided to give it a try. I got some photos taken and ended up doing a photo shoot for an ad at the department store where I was working. It wasn't a fun experience because the photographer kept yelling at me, and she had no idea I wasn't a trained model. I really wasn't thrilled with the process, and the anxiety over what I looked like was excruciating.

One day at work I had heard that John Casablancas, who owned one of the premiere modeling agencies in New York, was coming to town to scout for modeling talent. Everyone told me I should go, and I decided it couldn't hurt. I was always interested in fashion and was constantly reading all of the current fashion magazines. It was sort of a secret dream of mine, and as a teenager, when I would spend a lot of time by myself in my room, I would make myself up to look like the models in the magazine. Alone in my room I knew I could be a model, but out in the world was another story. So I gathered up my pictures and went to the audition. As we stood in line to meet with Mr. Casablancas, we could look through a glass window into the office where he was doing the interviews. When it got to be my turn he took his time looking through my pictures instead of quickly flipping through like he had done with the other girls. He commented that mine were pretty, that he liked what he saw. Then he told me to lose weight and go to New York. I was crushed because all I heard was the "lose weight" part, not the "go to New York" part.

When I walked out of the glass-bowl office, the other girls asked me what he had said because he had reacted differently to me than to all the other previous girls who went in there. I told them what he said, and they thought losing weight was no big deal because he probably tells everyone that. I was thin then, but not model thin, which was a whole other set of criteria. The other girls obviously saw my meeting as positive; all I could see was failure. Those words about my weight translated into "you're not good enough, no way could you be a model." I never saw what the others saw.

I felt such rejection that I let my secret dream go and never tried again. That was it, the end of a possible beginning of a life-changing career that I was too blind to see. I share this story because now I realize that it's not important how others see you, but how *you* see you. That's all that matters, and unless you get rid of that toxic bad self-image you will never see who you really are. A couple of years after that experience, I began to figure this out and began a transformational journey to find the real me. I'm still on that journey, and will be until I leave the Earth, but now I go out into the world fearlessly festooned and fabulous!

Frozen Peas

I've never been hungry. Growing up, we always seemed to have what we needed. We had food, and in between Mom's trips to the grocery store there would always be something stuck back in the freezer that you could pull out, heat up, and eat, even if it wasn't what you particularly wanted. Mom always had a bag of some sort of frozen vegetable in the freezer. Usually it was peas. Visit the home of someone who you know is doing well finan-cially and open their fridge. Odds are, it won't be empty. As soon as their stock of food gets low, they buy more. Their freezer always seems full too, so that bag of peas that has been there awhile rarely gets eaten because they just keep buying more freezer food, pushing that bag of peas to the back. It never gets so bad that they have to eat the peas. Well, there was a point in my life where the bag of peas that had been in my freezer forever was the only thing I had left to eat. Various circumstances had contributed to my dire financial situation, mainly a lull in my art commissions.

While I was savoring every spoonful of those little defrosted green balls of love, I was thinking how we become desensi-tized when we have so much. We just eat our food without really thinking about it. When you can go to the grocery store and fill your cart with whatever you want, you do that, just going through the motions. But when you're hungry and you don't have the money to go to the store, and you look in your empty fridge again with nothing there to eat, then you open your freezer and . . . *voila*! There it is! Through the freezer fog you discover that bag of peas like you had just found a pot of gold! Then, you go through the ritual of preparing them, ceremonially opening up the bag, placing the hard, frozen peas in a saucepan full of water, watching them heat up over the stove, your stomach anxiously awaiting their arrival. Although peas are not my favorite vegetable, on that day they were transformed into the best-tasting, most delicious food I'd ever had!

It's not fun to go through hard times, but that's when we learn the most about ourselves. I wouldn't trade my frozen pea experience for anything, because it helped me learn that my circumstances have nothing to do with who I am as a person. At the time, I felt bad about myself because of my lack of funds. Our culture tells us that success and worthiness equals having money. Yet that's not the truth. My brother, Doe Dave (we call him Doe Dave because when my niece was little she couldn't say "uncle" and it came out "Doe" so it just fit), always says to me, when I'm describing a tough moment happening in my life, "Ain't no big thing but a chicken wing!" One time when I needed brakes on my car and couldn't afford them he said, "Deb, don't you know? Stopping's optional!" Ha! Immediately it made me laugh, taking the heaviness and negative energy off of the situation, and lifting my mood. Eventually my circumstance worked itself out.

When I moved back to Cleveland in 2003, my brother was diagnosed with AIDS and his life began changing in devastating ways. His world as he knew it was crumbling. His wife was leaving him, and because of how physically sick he was, he had to leave his job. He had gotten two master's degrees and had worked so hard to get to where he was in his life, then in an instant it all was gone. Not only was he struggling with his mortality and just being physically being ill, he was also experiencing the devastating emotions associated with the stigma of that disease. There were times when I would go over to his apartment, put the key in the door, and not know if I was going to find a body. He was in a deep, dark place, and finding his way out seemed impossible. With Mom gone, I felt like I needed to be there, and so did my sister.

But in the midst of his darkness, I knew, he wanted to live. His doctor told him that no matter what, he could never skip taking his daily meds, and he followed those instructions. I did the best I could to try and be there for him. There were many days where my patience with his anger and attitude was tested immensely, but I hung in there because I love him and that's what you do. I was struggling financially after my move and didn't always have extra money, but I'd take my last twenty dollars and buy him a bag of groceries because he needed it more than me. Sometimes when I'd drop it off he would be so full of anger towards life that I would set down the plastic bag of groceries and say in a very loud voice, "You're my brother and I love you but right now you are being an asshole! So you're not going to see me for a couple of days because I'm taking a timeout, but I will be back because I will never abandon you!"

There were moments during those dark days where my Bone Lady world seemed juxtaposed to his struggle. Here I was, as the Bone Lady, spreading my message of "Be who you are," and he was finding the courage to do just that. I told him one day that I would take him to the AIDS Task Force to get a free bag of food and help with his rent from the Ryan White Fund. We drove there in the Bonemobile and parked right out front. Then both of us looked at each other, chuckling at how bizarre it was sitting there in the orange Volvo wagon with a giant bone on top! So much for not attracting attention to the fact that we were going into the AIDS Task Force! Sprinkled in amid the despair were absurd moments like this that would make us laugh, much like back when we were on the horrible cancer ride with our mom.

Doe Dave was starting to come out of the depths by seeing his doctor, taking his meds, and dealing with his changing life. Physically he was starting to feel stronger as his health was improving, but the support system that our government and community set up to help people who are ill was failing him, leaving us all to wonder if there wasn't some sort of underlying discrimination against AIDS patients. When he needed help the most, it wasn't available to him. Our family was not religious, but at one point my brother tried to seek counsel from a priest at a local church that will remain nameless; he was turned away because he wasn't a member of the church. Unbelievable! I can see how people without families who are sick end up homeless and on the street. For my brother, not getting the help he needed played on his psyche. "They're just waiting for me to die," he said.

His doctor at the Cleveland Clinic, though, was awesome, keeping him alive and keeping his spirits up because she had never lost an AIDS patient. When there was a glitch in his insurance, she would send him to the Free Clinic to get his meds. One time, I drove him over there to pick up his medicine. At the time I was being considered for a national Visa commercial and was constantly on the phone with the agents in Los Angeles. So while he went inside of the Free Clinic to get his meds so he could live, I was sitting outside in the parking lot on the phone with someone in L.A. discussing this commercial. He was in the darkest time of his life, and here I was, as the Bone Lady, getting all of these opportunities, which in my heart I didn't think I deserved anyway. Many times I found myself downplaying the good that was happening to me because it didn't seem fair that he had to go through all of this pain while so many doors were opening for me.

Over time, my brother started to get better, and the more he started to embrace his truth of who he is, the more his life really started to change. He went from dying from AIDS to living with it, and if you talk to him today he will tell you that AIDS was the best thing that ever happened to him, because it was the catalyst that led him to change his life and live authentically. AIDS is no longer the death sentence that it once was, and he is living proof of that. I've never seen anyone beat illnesses like he has, and even his doctors are amazed. His attitude and ability to laugh at life and himself were, and are, by far the best medicine. Now he has a wonderful life with his partner, they have dogs, a cat, a great house, and he still is the funniest person I know. His struggle gave him the blessing of knowing how to recognize what's really important in life and how not to sweat the small or the big stuff. I've certainly learned a lot from him, and just when I think I've heard every funny thing he could say, he comes up with something totally new, leaving me in tears with laughter!

He's also my "football buddy" (or my "Bitch about the Browns partner in crime")–and with what we Browns fans have gone through over the years, we all need one of those!

*   *   *

As Doe Dave's life was improving, mine continued to be full of ups and downs. As an artist, I was used to financial instability. But I had to get real with my living situation. Doe Dave and his partner lived down the street from me, and when they bought a house, they urged me to move into their former apartment. I could no longer afford the house I was living in, and moving to their apartment wasn't something I wanted to do, and in my gut it didn't feel right, but I did it anyway. A friend of mine was looking for a place, too, so we decided to be roommates and save some money. It worked out for a while, but then I ended up living there on my own.

I was painting, being the Bone Lady, and going to the games, and for a while things seemed to be going well, except then my personal life started to spiral downward. I thought my life would be better if I just had a man in it, and I wasn't making good choices with the men I chose to date, and emotionally it was taking its toll on my heart. Then Olive, my sweet cat who I had for eighteen years, passed away in my arms, leaving me devastated. I was working on a painting at the time, and that had a calming, healing effect on me. I think that was the first time when I connected my painting to a ritual of healing for my heart.

Not long after that, the relationship I was in ended in an abrupt, hurtful way, but after a little bit of time he and I continued to talk. No matter how I'm treated by someone, I always see the good in people. It's like I can see through whatever dark fog is around them that causes them to behave badly towards me, and then after the initial hurt has lessened I see the love they have in their heart. That's just who I am, although it's not always an easy process for me to go through because some people can take advantage of that. Sometimes I wonder if I tend to stay at the party too long because the memory of their breaking my heart would linger with me like red lipstick on a coffee cup that I couldn't wash off. Eventually the remnants would fade, but not without a lot of determined time spent scrubbing vigorously.

This particular guy had a really cool, unusual cat, and I had heard that the cat, for whatever reason, had ended up for adoption at a local pet store. Even though I didn't have the extra money, I drove out to the far east side of Cleveland and rescued him. He lived with me for a very short time until he got sick. I had to give him infusions every day, which after having to do that for Olive at one point in her life, I knew how to do. He didn't get better, though, and wasn't going to, so with the vet's urging I decided to let him go. I only had him for two months, but as I held him in my arms while he crossed over, I felt the sadness and love overwhelm me. I wondered why that whole devastating, sad experience had to happen. Then, one day, after a lot of time had passed, I realized that because I followed my urge to go rescue him, he hadn't died in a cage in a pet store but in my loving arms.

A month after that sad experience, my brother-in-law passed away suddenly. That time seemed like such a blur. Out of respect for the privacy of my sister and their kids I'm not going to elaborate on that story. All I will say is that he was such a big spirit in the room, and his transition to this day has left a huge void in our family that will never be filled. I tried the best I could to be there for my family, but with my own strength not being up to par it took every ounce of energy I had left just for me to deal with my own emotions, let alone theirs.

* * *

Things started getting a bit tough for the Bone Lady, too. I was still getting opportunities to wear my beehive and share her with the world, but difficulties started presenting themselves. Having growing public popularity is fun, but once in a while some sort of backlash occurs. Most of the fans liked that I was around, but on occasion someone would say something mean or disrespectful. Normally, I would just let it slide off my back. But as the Bone Lady's popularity rose, going to the games became overwhelming. I would arrive at the Muni lot and spend most of the morning posing for what seemed like hundreds of pictures while meeting fans. I loved doing it, but it was exhausting, and then by the time I walked into the stadium there would be another swarm of fans wanting pictures. I was, and am, always grateful when someone asks for a picture or autograph, and I'm always happy to oblige, but I didn't realize the amount of energy it took out of me every Sunday. The things that were happening in my personal life were already zapping my energy, and it took extra energy to be the Bone Lady. Sometimes I would skip the Muni lot and just go to the game, and people would be so disappointed that I hadn't been tailgating. I had become part of their game-day experience, and when I didn't show up it wasn't the same for them. I felt a responsibility to be there, and hated disappointing them, but the more the Bone Lady was growing in popularity, the more Debra was slipping further away.

There were times when I committed to appear at a charity event but didn't have the money to get there. That was tough. I had such a hard time charging for an appearance because I hadn't created the Bone Lady to make money and I didn't feel worthy of being paid for my time. There were so many occasions when I didn't know how I was surviving, but I just kept going. As I continued to be her, little pieces of Debra started to shine through, but there were moments when I would feel so raw and vulnerable putting myself out there that I almost couldn't function.

For some reason that inner voice that I had heard when I first created the Bone Lady was still so strong. Many times that voice was the only motivation I could muster to get me to "bone up." I think because the Bone Lady became popular so fast, getting so much attention from other fans and national and local media, that I never felt I'd actually earned the attention. It happened easily, and I didn't have to work at it, so I didn't feel like I deserved any of it. I was still carrying those old wounds, not thinking I was good enough, plus I was already struggling emotionally and financially in my personal life. Sometimes I didn't even want to leave my house, but I continued to go to the games. There, I would give one hundred percent, making others laugh and smile for hours, then drive home alone afterwards, peel off my Bone Lady outfit, and get in the bathtub to wash her away while crying in solitude. Oh, and watching all of that bad football surely didn't help!

For seven years, I bought my two tickets in the Dawg Pound from a guy who had bought eight seats when the Browns returned. He made a very good profit on me over the years, and even at one point started to advertise his other seats on eBay as a "Sit with the Bone Lady" experience. When I found this out, I told him he could continue to do that as long as he kept selling me my seats. Over those years I had made friends with everyone sitting around me, and I would use my extra seat to bring people to the game, bring other out-of-town fans, and even sometimes auctioned it off for charity. People got used to me sitting there, and if they wanted to meet the Bone Lady and get a picture, they knew where to find me. But at the end of one of the seasons, all of that changed when the guy who'd been selling me the tickets—and who'd even had me over for dinner with his family—turned into a real jerk, and stopped selling me my seats. At first I was devastated, especially because of my buddy Tim, who sat next to me, and other fans in the section who were now my friends. I couldn't figure out why all of a sudden he changed his tune, but all I could conclude was that he didn't like Bone Lady's rising popularity and wanted to find a way to cut me down.

After that season, I went to have my annual meeting with the Browns. I had become a sort of fan liaison, an "ambassador to the team," as a few people in the front office referred to me, so I would give them ideas on how to improve things for the fans and their game-day experience. Usually my ideas would fall on deaf ears, but I felt a responsibility to offer my services for the greater good of all fans. So when my ticket situation became an issue, I went to them. They had had no idea what I was having to deal with. They loved what I was doing as the Bone Lady, and that I was there at the games, so they offered me one seat elsewhere in the Dawg Pound, which I had to pay for. I couldn't come up with the money, but when I told my friend John Adams, who bangs a drum in the bleachers at every Indians home game, he said, "Bone Lady has to be at the games!" He paid for my seat that year.

That next season, I sat a couple of sections over in the Pound near some really nice people, except for one guy who sat next to me. The more beer he drank, the meaner he got, and I was the brunt of his assholery. I don't know if that's even a word but I once heard a friend use that term, and it describes this man's behavior. During a night game when we played the Broncos, a couple of Bronco fans came to see me during halftime. They knew the Barrel Man, Tim, who was the most well-known Bronco fan for a really long time, just like Big Dawg for the Browns. I knew him from the HOF and our PFUFA reunion, which he would come to every year. These two fans wanted a picture with me, but the jerk guy, who had just gotten back from getting his twentieth beer, stood there with his large arm in front of me, not letting me take a photo, and proceeded to yell "Bone Lady's a c---!" Are you kidding me? I apologized to the two Broncos fans, and then I commented that I was sure they have a couple of fans like that guy in their stadium because I'd been to a game in their stadium! The next season I told the Browns that I really couldn't go to the game by myself, so they moved my seats, giving me two tickets elsewhere.

I was running on fumes but kept going as if nothing in my life had changed. I have a very strong will, and I'm determined to persevere, but I also have a certain pride that can isolate me from others when things aren't going well. I'm usually there for my friends, but when I'm the one in need it's hard for me to ask for their help. Maybe I was depressed, but I certainly didn't think so at the time. Everything in life just got so big and over-whelming like a mountain I had stumbled upon but couldn't climb. I don't think I even dealt with my grief but instead threw it in the bag that I was carrying on my shoulders, and as time went on that bag got heavier and heavier. I hated the apartment I was living in. I tried to be grateful for it, but from day one when I moved in I had never liked living there. I was barely able to take care of myself financially and was losing the drive to keep going out to find painting jobs. Life was hard and any morsel of joy I had was soon sucked right out of me. I felt if I only had a man who loved me, all would be well. Little did I know that that old, buried wound from childhood would fool me into thinking that a man would fix everything. But I just wanted some kind of relief, an unconscious escape from my sadness. So when a man did appear, I immediately jumped all in without any regard for anyone else and didn't pay attention to my own gut feelings, which were screaming, "Don't go there!"

Then the most devastating event happened that literally sent me over the cliff without a lifeline. My beloved dog Molly passed away in her sleep after being with me for sixteen years. I'm tearing up as I write this because I miss her every moment of every day. If you've ever loved a dog and then lost it, you know exactly what I'm talking about. I don't mean to lessen the loss of a person that you love in your life, but this love with Molly was the purest, most unconditional love ever, like it was direct love from God.

She was a rescued dog that showed up one day when Tom and I had just moved into our house. A neighbor had scooped her up off of the highway shivering, terrified, and skinny. She couldn't even walk. We tried to find the owner but never did. This dog obviously had been through some sort of trauma or abuse, and all she wanted was for me to hold and hug her. At the time, Tom thought we couldn't have a dog because we traveled so much, but I remember saying to him, "Sometimes life isn't convenient, and people, beings, dogs just show up when they're supposed to." He ended up loving her as much as I did, and she became part of our family. She would go everywhere with us, riding in Tom's van all over the country while we picked antiques and visited friends and family. After Tom and I broke up, Molly went everywhere I went, traveling in the back of the Bonemobile on my way up to Cleveland and even on painting jobs. She was my best friend, surrogate child, constant companion, and she loved me no matter what. Every day when I opened the door, she was always so excited to see me. I commented once to a friend that I never had a guy be that excited when I'd come home!

So after Molly was gone and I had nothing left in my heart except for pain, I let this man swoop me up and take care of me. I will always appreciate that he was there for me, but I wasn't in any emotional state to be there for him. Had we met at a different time or under different circumstances maybe things would have turned out better for the two of us, but I had totally lost myself, forgetting who I was or what I loved. I erased my past by quitting everything that I loved—my painting, being the Bone Lady, going to Browns games . . . I even stopped seeing friends or family. I just couldn't handle the excruciating pain of loss in my heart, so I just slipped away for the next year like I had fallen down a hole.

LADIES LOVE FOOTBALL, TOO!

Did you know that almost *half* of all NFL fans are women, and 46 years old is the average age? Well now you do! Yet only in recent years has the NFL fully embraced its female fans. I don't know why it took so long, but I'm sure when sponsors and others saw there was money to be made, well—they were in. For so long ladies who love football had nothing to wear. All of the gear was made for men. You had the choice of an ugly t-shirt or sweatshirt that never fit right or a jersey that made you look like a linebacker. At least that's changed.

Soon, I hope that the NFL and the media that cover the games start to have more women involved. It would be nice for the criteria to be the same for women as for the men who cover it: based on their knowledge of the game and not their appearance.

Also, teams could really rethink their cheerleaders. I don't have an issue with women on the sidelines cheering, but do they have to look like strippers? Bumping and grinding like they are missing a dance pole? I am by no means a prude, I mean look at me and yes I have a message on my rear, but I have shorts on and I'm not half naked! Ladies embrace being sexy, but I think they could class it up a bit. When half of your customers are female I think it's kind of disrespectful. Many women are there to watch the game and don't want half-naked women grinding in front of them.

Now gentlemen, I know most of you are okay with that but my advice is to go to the game first and then go to the strip bar! Everything has a place and if the NFL wants this sport to be kid

friendly, then having stripper-like cheerleaders provocatively dancing in front of these kids really sends a wrong message. If I had a daughter and she went to the game, would I want her to aspire to that? Yes be a cheerleader, but how about tasteful ones who are really there to cheer wearing skirts and sweaters? Or a beehive and a hooped skirt? HA! How about male cheerleaders? You notice there aren't any Chippendale dancers on the sidelines. Hey, that would be inappropriate too!

When the Dallas Cowboys started the whole NFL cheerleader thing, it was the 1970s and the world was different for women. TV was all T&A ala *Charlie's Angels*. I know sex sells but the world is changing and how about showing respect towards your female fan base who are your customers? Why not have your daughter aspire to be like Sarah Thomas, the first NFL referee? **Let's support the new trails that are being blazed by women and not keep doing something because it's what we've always done.** Some women think they have to go along with our culture's standard of sex and beauty. Why not have women of all shapes, sizes, ethnicity, and age cheering on the teams? Even though sex sells, why not change the standard of what is sexy and not leave out women who don't "fit the mold"? Believe it or not, money is *never* the reason to do anything. Do it because it's the right thing to do. Integrity goes a long way. So let's change it up. Be a leader not a follower!

Ladies like to see a good-looking guy, too. But when it comes to a player on my team, I don't care what he looks like—I only want to know: Can he play?

The more You Know The More You See — Don't be Afraid to Ask Someone to Explain the Game

The more you know about the game of football the more fun you will have watching it. Whether you first started watching football as a kid, came to it later on in your life, or just started, it truly is a lot more fun when you know how it's played. I've noticed that people just assume everyone knows about it and sometimes it can feel intimidating to ask. For those of you who already know a lot about the game, be patient and don't make fun of those who are just learning. Once you have the basics down, you can then learn more by watching the game and when certain plays unfold or things happen, you can learn at those moments about that particular aspect of the game, rule, or play. I've learned to not ever be afraid to say, "I don't know" because you will never know everything. People who ask questions and are open to learning new things live the most enriched lives. Life for them is never boring!

For example, although you didn't ask me, if you did I might share a couple of my football pet peeves . . .

- What drives me *crazy* are celebrations in the end zone. Hand the ball to the ref like a professional.

- What drives me even *crazier* is when linemen over celebrate making a tackle. That's your job.

- Wouldn't it be nice to call a sports talk radio show and not be called "honey"? Look, I know that the guy doesn't mean anything by it, and I'm sure he's been saying it for years. He probably learned it from the generation before, but it is a little condescending. Does he call the older gentleman callers "molasses"?

Don't Ever Dim Your Light For Anyone!

To all of the women who love the game of football and to those who have been involved in the game, behind the scenes, covering it for the media, and those women who play or have played the game . . . I tip my beehive to you. WAY TO GO!

Apartment Number 4

I was in a dumpster at Crocker Park. That could figuratively describe my life at that time, but I literally was standing in a dumpster, pulling out used boxes to prepare for my move. After living my life for one year out in a suburb with the man who I'd let scoop me up and take me far away from my life as I'd known it, I was preparing to start a new one. My friend Art, one of the friends I didn't lose touch with at that time—actually, he relentlessly didn't let me lose touch with him—called me, "Bone in the 'burbs," knowing that I was as far from fitting in there as a square peg in a round hole. He knew that whole year was not what or how I should be living, but he wanted me to be happy so he didn't interfere. At that time I thought I was happy, but in reality I didn't have a clue what kind of life I wanted.

I had mostly stopped painting, just holding on to that part of my life by doing projects around the man's house where I was staying. My heart wasn't in it, and he was always in control of everything, so I never finished any of those projects, which led to him being angry at me. He was struggling with his own problems, and I was just another burden added to his pile of stress. I had lost all of my strength, and my grief for my dog Molly and missing my old life made me sad to the point where

I had days I couldn't even function. At his urging I tried to get a job and ended up with one at Crocker Park. It was the kind of job I might have taken when I was in my early twenties, but I was just grateful to have anything that got me moving out in the world. Even though the job was in the design field, it was what I call a "fake" job. You couldn't make any money at it, and you were set up to fail so that the company never had to pay you commission once you were trained. The turnover was constant.

Two months into the job one of my past clients from Columbus contacted me about working on an addition to their home, which I had helped them redo years earlier. They were angels sent from God. They offered me the kind of money I used to make which was great, but even better was the opportunity to once again use my gifts of painting and design. To have my work be so valued was the emotional boost I needed. Plus, the project gave me the ability to get my finances back on track. I decided to move and found a great place back in Lakewood, where I had lived before a detour into dysfunction took hold of me.

So there I stood in the dumpster behind the Crocker Park store where I was working, collecting a pile of flattened boxes, when suddenly I heard a woman yell, "Bone?" My friend Judy from Channel 19, whom I hadn't seen in a long time, was talking on her cell phone and I heard her say to the person on the other end, "Oh my God, I see Bone and she's in a dumpster at Crocker Park!"

The person on the other end was my friend Christine, also from Channel 19. I had lost touch with everyone, and no one really knew where I'd gone. I had disappeared from my old life, especially my Bone Lady world. Just as I was taking the steps back to that old life, here were my friends when I needed them. Christine told Judy to give me a hug. Judy hung up and insisted I come for dinner with her and her partner Dick, who I also just love. When you see friends that you haven't seen in a long time, who you love dearly, the moment you see them again you realize that the love you share as friends never goes away just because time has separated you. I felt so loved and supported by Judy and Dick, like I had run out of gas and just got refueled.

Before I left their house, Judy asked me if she could tell people at the station she'd seen me. "Of course," I said. "Better yet, tell them you saw Bone Lady in a dumpster at Crocker Park, and then just leave it at that! People have been wondering what ever happened to her! Ha! Let them come to their own conclusions!"

I moved into the most wonderful apartment near the lake, apartment number 4. It had hardwood floors, tall ceilings, lots of space, and it was in an older building with original moldings and doors and an old screen door in the back. Sometimes we get what we ask the Universe for, even if we don't realize we're asking for it. Sometimes I think we assume that the only gifts or miracles from the Universe (God) are big substantial ones that take away all of our struggles and challenges in life. Because we aren't winning the lottery or marrying a movie star, we think the Universe must hate us because we aren't getting what we want. We are receiving gifts and miracles all of the time, but because they seem small and insignificant, we don't count them. The day I realized I did get what I had asked for, my outlook changed for the better. I started to notice the little daily miracles—like apartment number 4, with the old gray screen door, just like I had asked for.

The transition into my new life was busy. I was unpacking and settling into my new home while commuting to a client's house in Columbus and also continuing at the Crocker Park job. Eventually something had to give. One day I simply never returned to the job at Crocker Park. It was the kind of place where management tried to control your every move. At one point, I was questioned for using the bathroom, not realizing I had to ask permission. I then raised my hand like a kid in school wanting to be called upon, and loudly asked the regional rep, "Can I use the bathroom now?" I'm sure that pissed her off, but I found that whole company atmosphere, the loss of identity and dignity, completely absurd. They didn't pay enough to own me even though they treated me that way. So the "fake" job had to go!

For about a year I spent the majority of my time in Columbus. My clients and their family were so good to me, and they sort of took me under their wings as I painted for them and also built my strength and confidence back up. I will never ever forget their friendship and support. For my birthday that year they even gave me the iPad on which I'm typing this book, because I didn't have a computer.

My sister had given me a gift certificate for a Reiki session with a friend of hers. I'd been a spiritual seeker since my early twenties, beginning with a trip to New York to learn how to meditate. Something inside of me always knew there was more to life than just what we see and experience. I would read all of the current books on spirituality and New Age thinking, taking with me what resonated and "felt right." Throughout the years my spiritual practice waxed and waned, going full force when things were tough and I felt I needed support, but slacking when life was good. The Reiki session helped integrate my spiritual practice with my life's daily routine—it became just like brushing my teeth and taking a shower.

I was meditating every day, at least twice a day, taking sea salt lavender baths in the big old bathtub in my apartment, doing yoga regularly, and reading everything I was guided to read about my spiritual practice. I wanted to clear out my channel to the Divine and receive messages and guidance more clearly, so I stopped drinking alcohol and coffee for about two years. I learned about the various tools that could help me connect to

Spirit (my higher self), like the Angels, tarot and Angel cards, crystals and smudging, nature and animal totems, Earth magic and other worldly beings, Native American spiritual practices, the Ancestors. I didn't just pick them but let them appear in my life and then paid closer attention to what resonated with me. It felt like spirits had taken my hands and walked with me down this road as I was being shown my true purpose here on the Earth.

So many synchronistic events were happening to me and seemed to be multiplying as I walked my spiritual path. I don't believe in coincidences, and when something like it occurs I believe it's merely a message or a sign pointing you in the right direction. We aren't living our lives alone, we have spiritual guides that walk with us, helping us if we just ask. Some guides are Angels, Archangels, Ancestors, Ascended Masters, Nature Beings, or Animals, and I had felt their presence since I was a kid but I wasn't aware of the help they could give me because I didn't know I had to ask for their help. Once I realized this, they began showing up more often during my meditation practice, and I was able to develop a relationship with them by connecting on a daily basis. This for me has been life-changing, and I've been able to help others connect to their own spirit guides. Sometimes people appear in your life for a moment, serving as a guide, and then they're gone. This happened to me.

"Oh My God I think I just met a soul mate!" I thought while driving home from a New Year's Eve ceremonial gathering. I was overwhelmed by a feeling of already knowing this man deeply after simply shaking his hand and saying hello for the very first time. It was a strange, powerful feeling that left me unnerved. My gut ached like I had been punched in the stomach. I wasn't expecting to meet anyone that evening, let alone someone who affected me that powerfully. I had met soul mates before, but this meeting was on a far more intense level. It almost left me incapacitated, making driving home difficult. I hadn't had such a powerful meeting ever with another human. I felt pulled to him like metal to a magnet.

I decided not to ignore this intensity but trust that I was being led by Spirit to know this man. We both came to the conclusion that our meeting was divinely orchestrated, and we proceeded to see one another on a regular basis. During and after our encounters, creativity erupted out of me like lava pouring down the side of a volcano. Every idea or thought that had been lying dormant within me, maybe for years, was being brought to the surface as we engaged in what I will call a sort of spiritual healing practice. I was grounding myself into the Earth while connecting to the cosmic heavens. Paintings were flowing out of me like I was a conduit of spiritual expression. I set up all of my paints and canvases in my dining room, along with an altar of spiritual tools, and with all of the creative forces bursting out of me as I painted, the walls in my apartment seemed to expand. Not only was I painting but I was writing words that seemed to be channeled through me, journaling my experiences every day along with reading whatever I was guided to read. I felt like my soul was being opened up wide without any fear or condition being put upon what was coming forth creatively. It was like Spirit had been waiting for me my whole life—I had opened the door and was now downloading a lifetime of spiritual knowledge.

I know that some of you reading this may be thinking, "whack job." All I can say is that I feel compelled to share my real story, and speaking my truth, no matter how "out there" it may seem, is part of my journey while on this planet.

"What does all of this have to do with the Bone Lady," you ask?

Well, this awakening to my higher self (spirit, creator) was what led me back to being the Bone Lady again. For two years it had been painful for me to think about my past. Gradually, I found the courage to look back with a forgiving and grateful perspective. I had abandoned most of my artistic life, especially being an itinerant limner, and had pretty much stopped doing any historical, traditional style of painting. Maybe I'd abandoned that style of painting because it was so connected to my mom and it made me sad to return to it without her here. Whatever the reason, it wasn't conscious, but as I continued with this spiritual healing practice I was also able to return to my artistic life as a limner and eventually back to my Bone Lady world.

During this time of my spiritual seeking and awakening, I learned that the numbers 4, 44, and 444 are Angel numbers, and when you see those numbers they want you to know that they are walking with you always, supporting you along your path with much love. As my journey unfolded, the frequency of seeing these numbers throughout each day increased tenfold, reassuring me that I wasn't alone. And then one day I realized that all of my healing, spiritual unfolding, and reconnection back to Spirit—back to my true self—occurred in apartment number 4. It felt like I was living in a sacred portal: all that had occurred previously in my life, the good and the challenging, led me to this awakening of my destiny. As my reason for being here on the Earth at this time was revealed to me, I found out that being the Bone Lady was always a part of the plan.

Bone Lady Shoes

"It is by going down into the abyss that
we recover the treasures of life. Where you
stumble . . . there lies your treasure."
—Joseph Campbell

The Universe kept showing me that I was meant to be the Bone Lady by bringing me opportunity after opportunity. Even though I didn't feel worthy of all the attention, I decided to put on the beehive wig and go back out into the world. I had Bone Lady shoes, yet I hadn't ever truly believed I could fill them.

During my unannounced Bone Lady hiatus, I concluded that when you are meant to do something in this world it *is* easy and life just flows like the Universe is unfolding your destiny. All you have to do is lean back and ride the current instead of fighting it by thinking you're not worthy. As I got stronger within myself while doing my spiritual work in apartment number 4, I was able to appreciate the path I walked as an artist and as the Bone Lady and then was able to embrace both as part of my life's journey. Because the Bone Lady began as a thought that popped into my head, she was given to me by Spirit and for some reason I was meant to be this character. From day one of her creation my motto had always been "Be Who You Are." Now I was amazed to realize that her true purpose wasn't just about football but to help others have the courage to be their true selves.

For the next couple of years I'd lie on my couch in my apartment number 4 sanctuary and watch the Browns play football. Even though my beehive was packed away in the closet, my love and interest in the game of football didn't go away. The only thing I did keep active was my Bone Lady Facebook page, posting on it on rare occasions. I constantly listen to sports radio, and when someone would mention they saw the Bone Lady at a game it would make me laugh. They must've been hallucinating or having some sort of weird Bone Lady vision because I wasn't there, I was lying on my couch!

While I was in the midst of living in that dark hole, I was forced to confront the deepest wound of my life, my lack of self-worth. I couldn't believe that after all of the years I had spent in therapy, all of the self-help books I had read, all of the knowledge I had gained about healthy relationships and all of the years seeking spiritual truth, I still carried that same wound I'd had since I was a kid. I guess I thought that I had already healed it because I had worked so hard and so long on my issues. Maybe I needed that dark experience of not being me in order to find me and to appreciate and love myself, but now I needed a sort of final, huge healing that would rock me to my core. All of the grief, loss, and challenges turned out to be the biggest blessings of my life because those experiences brought me to my knees, stripping me down to the core of my true self where I could finally transform into the real me. Every decision that I ever made in my life was based on how I felt about myself at the time. When I felt really good about myself I made better, healthier, stronger choices for my life, but when I was feeling low and empty of any love for myself I would reach for something that would fill me up to make me feel better. That's when I usually made those not-so-good choices for myself, and it usually involved a man.

So it seems fitting that it took the man who was my soul mate like no other to help me reconnect with my past and embrace my higher self. Then, he abruptly walked out of my life as fast as he walked in. He wasn't meant to stay. The deep soul connection that I felt with him was real, yet once that had served its purpose, his leaving my life finally ripped off any band-aids that I had put on my wound of self-loathing.

When I had just moved into my new apartment number 4 and my spiritual journey was rapidly unfolding, I had gotten a sterling silver angel wing necklace that I wore to celebrate my emerging life purpose. During the year that my soul mate and I were together, I would always take it off so as not to break it when we were engaging in spiritual healing activity. One time when I went to put it back on I couldn't find it and for months it was missing until the day he left my life. After that final meeting with him I returned home to find my angel wing necklace sitting out in the open on the dresser in my bedroom as if it had been there all along. I immediately knew that getting my necklace back was a gift from Spirit, just as he had been. So with tears and sadness overwhelming me, I ceremoniously put it back on around my neck, clasping it tightly, and I've never taken it off since, even when I am dressed as the Bone Lady.

Shortly after that day, and while I was dealing with my heartbreak, the floodgates opened with Bone Lady opportunities. For almost three years, with my beehive packed away in the closet, nothing had happened. I never officially told anyone that I wasn't doing the character anymore. Maybe my energy wasn't in it any longer, and so everything stopped as I was on my Bone Lady hiatus. So why now were these opportunities coming? Did I need to have the experience of going away, then healing and becoming stronger, before I continued to be the Bone Lady? Or did I need to totally give her up in order to get to her true purpose?

The news director at Channel 19, who I had freelanced for in the past, called and wanted me to "Bone up" and have lunch with the Tailgate 19 guys and the sales staff on a Monday. That Friday evening before that meeting, I was walking on my street and there was Dan the news director, whom I hadn't seen in three years. He said they wanted me to be on the show hosting our Tailgate 19 party sponsored by Yuengling Brewery; I would be interacting with fans, giving away prizes, and talking about the game. I had been wanting to do this for a very long time and now it was being offered. I had always envisioned the Bone Lady doing this and I'm very comfortable on camera, but when you are trying to do something that no one has done before— well, you get frustrated by constantly being told no. Bone Lady doesn't look like the typical news or sports reporter, so trying to be on camera while wearing a beehive hasn't been easy!

Then within that very same week I got a call from the Browns and ended up meeting with Kevin Griffin, the new vice president of fan experience and marketing. He arrived on a Thursday from Seattle and called me on Monday to have lunch. I told him in all of the past years no one at the Browns had ever called me that quickly for a meeting! The floodgates of opportunities had indeed opened.

I rarely logged onto my Bone Lady Facebook page, but since I was coming back I thought I better check in. There were several messages from a guy named David Lee Morgan. He was trying to reach me because one of his friends was contracted to do an ESPN *30 for 30* film on Cleveland and the fifty-year championship drought. I called up David Lee and we had the most enthusiastic chat ever! I found out that he had worked as a sportswriter for the *Akron Beacon Journal* and had written a book on LeBron

James's high school years. He met Kris Bellman while covering LeBron because Kris was working on his film called *More than a Game*, also about LeBron's high school career. Kris happened to be in town from L.A. so we met and had lunch and immediately hit it off. He filmed me for the *30 for 30* during that season of my return. The film never came out but David Lee was the one who encouraged me to write this book and introduced me to David Gray, the publisher. Both just unexpectedly showed up in my life like they dropped out of the sky.

My return that season was like I hadn't ever left. Guys who'd written articles about me years earlier just called out of the blue for interviews. Strangely, they hadn't even known I'd taken time off. I was a little nervous about how my fellow Browns fans would feel about my return. They not only welcomed me back but told me over and over how much they had missed the Bone Lady. They embraced me like never before. Many game day Sundays, tears welled up in my overly made-up Bone Lady eyes and it wasn't from how the Browns were playing. Ha!

I was back, and this time it wasn't just about football because I now knew the underlying reason for the Bone Lady. It was to be out among people, helping them have the courage to be their true selves, too; to not to be afraid to be who they are. Empowering people while wearing a beehive was now my mission, and I was determined to bring the fun while doing it!

So You Want to Be an Ultimate Fan . . .

There isn't a handbook to teach you how to be an Ultimate Fan (it tends to just happen), but here are a few things I've learned along the way . . .

- One way to go if you are CREATIVE, CRAFTY, and, well, kinda CRAZY—*make your own outfit*. Don't knock it until you've tried it. If you choose this route you need to be prepared for what might follow. Look at my journey, I had *no* idea that a beehive wig would change my life, but it did. Oh, that and a glue gun! So if you embark down the path of character fandom I have a few lessons I've learned along my own fan journey. No two fan experiences are alike, so if I can help you out with what I've learned then I'm here to pass along some "Beehive Wearing Wisdom!"

- *You can't just paint your face, wear a mask, or put on a funny outfit* and decide you're going to be an Ultimate Fan or a Super Fan. Having an agenda to create a character will be fun for a moment, but it won't last because it's not authentic. Do something because you love it and just want to have fun. Then if it turns into something it will have happened organically and it will take you where it's meant to go.

- If your journey gets to be too much, know that *you are the one in charge* and you can say no. I was so honored when people would ask me to do appearances that I said yes to everything but over the years it wore me out.

- *Know that if you dress up in a character outfit you will attract kids.* Kind of like Mickey Mouse. So if your main objective in

tailgating is to drink and be two sheets to the wind, skip the dress-up part. Kids will want to meet you and get a picture, so it's just not cool to be hammered.

- *Always be kind and gracious even if you're being harassed* by opposing teams fans or overserved ones. Know that if you wear a wacky outfit you may attract the wrong kind of attention. Best to just let it roll off your back (or beehive in my case). If you aren't a kind person without the costume on, you won't be with it on. So if you're kind of a jerk and like to get into fights, don't be a character fan.

- *Give of yourself to help others.* That has been the most

rewarding part of being an Ultimate Fan. When you realize that you have the power to make someone smile and laugh, that is the best feeling EVER! So find a charity that means something to you personally or let it find you. Imagine how the world would change if every person gave of themselves for one cause to help others, animals, or the planet.

- *Be yourself* and let your true self shine through. Don't take yourself to seriously. It's fun, remember?

- *Be respectful of the other fans*, those from other teams and from your own team. Wearing a costume doesn't make you a better fan than other fans. Honor the fans who were there before you.

- *Take a friend with you* as it can be hard to go it alone. I found out that I couldn't go to the games alone as I needed someone to sort of watch out for me, run interference, and usually snap the pictures. It can get old for them real fast so have back up.

I created the Bone Lady just for fun, but I came to realize it was a responsibility. After being honored at the Hall of Fans, that responsibility grew as I realized I was representing Browns fans and our city of Cleveland.

What Will I Wear?

I made my outfit without a lot of thought, but over the years I learned a few things I can now share with you about fan garb. If you want to be creative and adorn yourself in expressing your team pride, here's a list of tips for you to think about.

- Decide how you want to express yourself, let your mind wander and don't be afraid to go for it. Do what feels right for you.

- Think twice before attaching your persona to a specific

player. With free agency your player might be on another team, so keep that in mind.

- Chose something unique yet timeless. You have no idea how long you might be doing this, so, as with fashion, classic and timeless always works. (I can hear my friends laughing now: "Bone Lady—classic and timeless?")

- Ladies, it's fine to be sexy but watch the vulgar "Halloween gone slutty" outfits. There's a time and a place for that. I'm not just suggesting this because kids are around but if your character takes off you could be doing this for 30 years and do you really want to be wearing those skimpy leather hot pants then? Think about it. (Again my friends are laughing!)

- Make an outfit that is adjustable for the weather. Extra layers for cold, some kind of rainproof gear. Sensible footwear is always a great idea! (My friends again are thinking, "platform shoes are sensible?")

- Decide how long you want to spend getting ready on game day. I know some people who paint their face and it takes hours. If you don't mind it taking that long then turn it into your game-day ritual and get mentally geared up for the game!

- Make sure your outfit is comfortable because you will be in it for a while. Make adjustments as you go along. I did and I've got it down to where it works for me.

Some people upon meeting me have asked if I was the REAL Bone Lady? . . . I reply . . . "Oh no! You mean there's another one?"

Dealing With Overserved Fans

Yes, sometimes manners go out the window when too much alcohol is consumed. Most fans are great and they just want to hug on you and get a photo. If you are dressed up in your

fan regalia you have to be prepared for attracting some of the overserved and obnoxious fans. I am always of the mindset to just let whatever disparaging comment they yell at you roll off your back. I never want to poke the bee's nest as I am not a fighter but a lover. But once in awhile I just have to say something as I can't resist. Here are a few scenarios:

- A good standard line is "Oh . . . your mother must be SO proud!"

- Once a very inebriated young man yelled, "Bone Lady . . . You're a sellout!" At first it caught me off guard and I thought, if he only knew that I could barely afford my game ticket and I had to scrounge for money to park. Instead of stating my case I just replied "Ahhh . . . WELL YEAH! Sure beats hookin'!" Everyone around cracked up and he just went away.

- Some guys think that because you're friendly and dressed as you are they can just have a touching free-for-all. If they ask to do inappropriate things I usually say "NO! . . . But thanks for asking!"

Is the Man of My Dreams in the Muni Lot?

I've gotten many marriage proposals in the Muni lot! For the young twenty-somethings I usually say, "If I could've possibly given birth to you, I can't date you!"

To the REALLY overserved gentlemen who profess "I LOVE you Bone Lady!" I'll reply, "How many beers HAVE you had? . . . cuz I'm not going to look very good to you in the morning."

For some reason the Bone Lady is like a chick magnet with many over-served female fans wanting to hug and hang on me just like the guys. Hey love is love. Some of my male buddies started to hang around when they realized this fact. Who knew the Bone Lady would make a great wingman.

The Greatest Gift You Can Give to Yourself Is to Give to Others

You express your love for your team by making a cool, fun outfit. You start to get attention from other fans and soon something is starting to grow but you're just not quite sure what. You keep showing up and doing it because it's fun. Then one day it dawns on you that you could really do some good work in the world by helping others. So that love you have for your team starts to sprout branches and soon those branches are touching many lives in many different directions.

Here are some things to think about when you have that desire to use your creation for the highest good.

- Think about what is meaningful to you and what may have touched your life. Look into your heart for the answer. Then proceed to find a charity or organization or individuals that need your help. Many times those will find you as the more you are out in the community you will be asked to participate in charitable causes.

- You can always go and see kids and put a smile on their faces. Find local hospitals, children's homes, shelters, schools, neighborhood groups.

- Get involved with other fans of your team. The Browns have one of the largest sports fan organizations in the world with almost 300 chapters. Most of them do charity work in their respective communities and it is a great way for the Browns to weave a thread of helping others around the world.

- Get to know fans from other teams. You will find that many of them are experiencing what you are and giving of themselves in their town. Started in 1999, with the first class honored in the Visa Hall of Fans at the Pro Football Hall of Fame, those fans wanted to have a reunion every year in Canton. So they formed Pro Football's Ultimate Fan Association. Each year the new class that was honored was invited to be a part of PFUFA. In 2006 the Visa Hall of Fans ended but PFUFA lives on. They still meet every year for a reunion during Hall of Fame weekend in Canton, Ohio. That's a great way to meet some other fans from other teams.

• Be self-sufficient; don't rely on your NFL team to be supportive of you. All teams are different and embrace their Ultimate Fans in various degrees or not at all. So you will have
to navigate that for yourself. I've learned that with anything
in life it is best for you to be at the helm steering your own
ship. The more popular your persona becomes, the more you
will attract all kinds of people who want you to do things for
various reasons. Best not to get caught up in their agenda
and stay on your own course. Do what feels right for you
and if it seems too good to be true, well you know the rest
of that saying!

Remember, if it's no longer fun . . . you don't have to do it. The
best thing I did when this Bone Lady ride got out of control was
to take a timeout. I didn't have to make any declarations, I just
went away for a while, reflected about the journey I was on, and
took the time to replenish myself. I gained much-needed clarity
and when my journey started up again, I was stronger, empow-
ered, and very focused about why I was doing it and where I
wanted to go. *Just because you've done something for a long time
and others want you to keep going doesn't mean you have to. You
have the choice to continue or not.* If you can't decide, then a
timeout is a great option as you will find the answer.

Now go root for your team and have fun!

Optimistic Sunday, Pessimistic Monday

Doesn't "hope springs eternal" describe every week during football season? Especially for Browns fans. We start out the season with hope and optimism because every team has a chance and we wonder if this year is our year. Then after losing the opening game (yes Browns fans, we usually do), we're snapped out of our optimistic coma and back to the reality of football. We are then on the ride of a football season—Sundays full of promise, too many Mondays full of disappointment and despair. No other fan knows this feeling better than a Browns fan.

I know people say "it's just a game," but here in Cleveland it's much more than that. Sports in this town weaves itself throughout our lives, entangling each defining sports moment with our own personal life story. It connects families, friends, coworkers, and even strangers throughout the course of a day, whether we are at a game, watching it on TV, or discussing it during the off-season. It's the lifeblood of our city, win or lose, and it is what defines our city's legacy and determines how we feel about ourselves as a city.

*   *   *

Growing up in Cleveland, Ohio in the 1960s and 1970s there wasn't a lot to be proud of. Around the country people referred to us as "The Mistake on the Lake" and on some level we believed it. But during that time there was one entity that was a part of our city that we were always proud of. That was our Cleveland Browns. They represented *us*, *our* city and they were a part of who we defined ourselves to be. Sports in this town *is* how we feel about ourselves. It goes way beyond a game—it's our history, our tradition, a thread that weaves through generations and is what makes Cleveland Cleveland. People from other cities have a hard time understanding that. Here sports feel different. We are emotionally connected especially to our Browns. They seep into our bloodstream when we are very young, turning the color to brown and orange. (That is, if you were raised right and not dropped on your head, hence becoming a Steelers fan!)

Our parents who were here in the 1950s and early '60s know what it feels like to win. They got to experience winning a championship. But for most of us who are too young to remember 1964 or weren't born yet, we have no idea what it feels like to win it all. Sure we won playoff games during the Kardiac Kids and the Bernie Kosar years, but we never even got to the big dance, let alone won it all.

Marianne Williamson has a fabulous quote: "Our deepest fear is not that we are inadequate. Our deepest fear is that we are powerful beyond measure. It is our LIGHT not our darkness that most frightens us." Maybe as a city we are afraid of our "light," "our success." We need to ask ourselves, "Do we feel worthy of winning a championship?" I mean deep down in our hearts? DO we honestly feel we can compete against anyone and win? We've all seen teams or individual athletes who weren't expected to succeed end up doing just that because of their strong belief in themselves.

We look back on the Bernie years with such high regard,

but when those games were happening, there was always doubt about winning, leaving us to conclude that the outcome was due to a lack of luck or some kind of doomed fate that "only happens in Cleveland." Honestly, I think in a lot of those games during that time, we were "surprised" when we did win instead of "knowing" that we would. That attitude still prevails with all of our sports teams in Cleveland. In this town we collectively hold our breath.

It doesn't help that the national media remind us over and over about the bad parts. Why is it whenever there is any big Cleveland sports news they have to show, once again, The Drive, The Fumble, Red Right 88, The Move, The Shot, The Decision? In Cleveland we *lived* through those painful moments. We don't need to be constantly reminded. It would be like being at your second wedding and watching a video of your "First Marriage," "The Divorce," "The one that got away," "The one who dumped you for your friend" . . .

*   *   *

When the Browns left Cleveland for Baltimore our hearts were ripped out. It was like a devastating divorce. When they returned in 1999, feeling like a jilted lover, I protected my heart by not giving them all of my emotions even though I was so excited that they were back.

I've spoken to other fans who felt the same way and we were just happy to have a team again in which we could keep the name, history, colors and traditions. Those early years after the Browns came back we were optimistic, but I think we were still living in the past, expecting the team to be good, like we kept sporting that mullet we wore in the eighties during the Bernie years when we had a competitive team and got close to the Super Bowl. We should've gotten a new haircut.

Over the past fifteen years we've had to take off our orange-colored glasses and face reality. I'm all about being positive and optimistic but not to the point of being delusional. Optimism and hope can keep you going thinking about the future, but soon reality stares you in the face. The fact is the Browns were an expansion team when they returned and not a very good one. Then impatience took over and the revolving door of new regimes, new coaches, new players, new front office personnel and eventually a new owner meant that no solid foundation was ever built. Consistency was nowhere to be found and with most fans living for the draft we kept looking for a superhero player to save the day (and maybe we still are). Oh and the bad football we've had to endure, with every once in awhile an exciting win thrown in to keep us hooked.

In my dating life my motto is, "It's not what you say but what you do." Words without actions are just words. With football being a big corporate business, you have men in suits speaking a lot of words during premeditated press conferences so they say a lot of things. I got tired of these various regimes telling me what they were going to do and how they were the right one to fix this team's culture of losing. Then they would leave town and the next guy would show up, clean house, and give us the same spiel about how they would be the one to turn it around.

When I'm out talking with other Browns fans they all have a very personal story to tell about their connection with the team. Sure it will be a great day when we finally win that Super Bowl, but who knows when that will be? (Hopefully before I die!) The most frustrating thing about being a fan is that we have no control over any decisions the team makes on or off the field.

There will always be a disconnect between fans and the team because it is no longer just about the game of football. For those of us fans who love the game and are emotionally connected to our team, the big business of football will always keep that disconnect going. Yes, winning does solve a lot, but with only one team winning the Super Bowl every year, winning is a temporary fix. With a combination of free agency and the impatience for a winner resulting in coaches moving from team to team faster than speed dating, the only constant is the fans. One day I hope that the ones in charge of the business of professional football realize that fans aren't just customers for them to sell tickets and merch to, resulting in them not caring whose butts are in the seats, but to embrace, appreciate, and validate the emotional legacy that we have to our team, our family, our city.

Ultimately, what we get out of being fans is up to us. Maybe this city needs to heal some emotional wounds in order to strengthen its self-esteem. On some level we don't feel like we are worthy or good enough, always comparing Cleveland to other cities. We are *so* hungry to win a championship, yet our moments of adversity and heart-wrenching disappointments have fed our negative appetites. Instead of focusing on what we're lacking, it's time to change our thoughts into positive ones and satisfy our hunger by embracing what we *love* about ourselves, our city. Let's celebrate what makes us unique and special. That elusive championship will arrive some day when we aren't holding on so tightly to the outcome. Things tend to come to you when you let them go and enjoy the moment.

Someone once asked me if I had known that the Browns would be a losing team since they came back would I have still been the Bone Lady? My answer was and is a definite "YES!" Because whether it's football or life in general, it's not about the destination but the journey—and what an amazing crazy wild beautiful journey it's been.

GO BROWNS!

Postscript

Thank you for reading my book! You probably didn't think you would learn about life's journey from a woman who loves football and wears a beehive wig and a hooped skirt with bones glued all over it! I appreciate your taking the time to read it or at least flip through its pages. If you see me out among the people somewhere, sometime, please come up and say hello. I would love to meet you.

I once met a very enlightened older man at a talk in Columbus. When it was time to say goodbye, I said, "Joe, it was so nice to meet you!" He replied in a startling way, "I'm so glad *you* had the opportunity!" That, my friends, is what *real* self-love and self-esteem look and sound like. I wish that for you.

—Bone Lady

BONE LADY'S OUTFIT

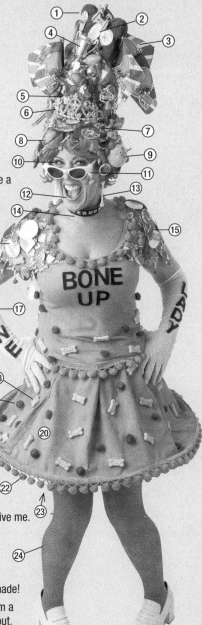

1. I made the fabric bone on top.

2. Some old collectible Browns buttons.

3. Flags from the Flag Lady Columbus Ohio.

4. Trophy—everyone needs one!

5. Wig—it weighs approximately 4½ lbs. (I have a coat hanger inside so my hair stands erect.)

6. Tiara. I was the Bone Queen in the Miss Ohio Parade.

7. Buttons are photos of tailgate buddies. I wore them to the Super Bowl; it was like taking friends along.

8. Little footballs from the infamous Yankee Trader in Columbus, Ohio.

9. Snowman from Christmas Parade. (I'm like those people who leave their Christmas lights up all year long.)

10. False eyelashes.

11. Glasses. I can't see out of them! I need readers.

12. Orange lipstick. L'Oreal has the perfect shade.

13. Bone earrings, painted white.

14. Dog collar—duh!

15. Funny pins. One favorite: "I'd kick your ass, but this is my best dress!"

16. Browns pins, Cleveland pins, things people give me.

17. Evening gloves, of course.

18. Milk Bone dog biscuits.

19. Brown balls are just brown balls.

20. Outfit is dyed Rit Tangerine orange. It's my shade!

21. Hula Hoop sewed into skirt—best advice from a drag queen when I wanted my skirt to stick out.

22. Dingle balls, hand-dyed.

23. Orange biker shorts on under skirt; message on rear.

24. White fishnet stockings, dyed orange.

25. White spray-painted platform shoes.

Photo: Jesse Kramer

Bone Lady is what happens when you drink too much beer and own a glue gun. (Kids, don't try this at home—the beer part, that is!) If there really was a Fashion Police I'm sure I would've been arrested a long time ago!

- I'm always making new outfits because I can't wash them. After a while I start to smell a little ripe! You can only "Febreze" yourself so often. If the Bone Lady had a fragrance, it would be called "Game Day" and it would smell like a combination of Febreze, wet dog bones, spilled Dawg Pound beer, and smoke from the tailgate. Oh, and my Chanel Madamoiselle!

- My motto: "If anything falls off, just pick it up and put it back on!"

- The first time I wore my outfit, when I got home I left the skirt sitting on the floor. My dog Molly ate the biscuits off, glue and all. I quickly learned to hang up my clothes.

- Once I was asked by a national radio host if EVERYTHING on the Bone Lady was "real"? I knew what he was referring to and my retort was "YES . . . well . . . everything except the hair!"

- I used to change the buttons on the back of my wig every season so the guys sitting behind me would have new reading material.

- Once, while riding in a cab on our way to do the Jimmy Kimmel Show, Mikey T. Boss Hogette, in his dress and pig nose, looked over at me while I was putting on my white Bone Lady shoes and asked, "Why aren't your shoes orange?" In all of my Bone Lady garb, I look over at him and said, "You don't know anything about fashion!"

A Huge List of Hugs, Thank Yous, and Lots of Love!

First I want to thank you for buying this book. Actually my landlord would like to thank you personally and give you a big hug!

Second, I want to thank every person who has ever crossed my path in a good way or in a not-so-good way, for all of you were mirrors in which I could learn about myself.

Third, a thank you to all Cleveland Browns fans everywhere! You have embraced me and shown me such love. I even thank the overserved ones who weren't so nice to me!

Also . . . I have to say thank you to David Lee Morgan—without his encouragement and suggestion I write this book, it never would've been written! "Myyyyyy Friend" Jim Madden who has always kept me on my path even when it was tough, you're my Angel on Earth! My whole family here on the Earth especially Doe Dave and my Seeeester and my family on the other side. Meemaw, I miss you! Tom Delach, one of my favorite people on the planet. Our time was well spent! Chris Reynolds, thanks for connecting with me in this life and reminding me what I already knew about myself but had forgotten. Don Doskey, another soul mate teacher in my life. Karen Gurney, my warrior sister. To Bill Mitchell now on the other side. Michele Ziegler and Roseann Heinrich for being with me on my Angel journey. All of my friends past and present, you know who you are. I love all of you always and am so grateful for our paths crossing for you are indeed gifts to my life—xoxo! To all my fellow Browns fans and former tailgate buddies. I had a blast on this ride! To everyone at Gray & Company and to Frank Lewis, thank you for your patience. To my right hand middle finger who was such a warrior while typing this book one letter at a time on my iPad! Cousins Laura and Gary Dumm for your illustrations and support. Jesse Kramer for your cover photo. Dan Rizzie for your beautiful portrait. All of my friends who contributed with photos especially Packalope, Big Nasty, Mr. and Mrs. Seahawk, Arrowman, Howiette, cousin Kathy, Michele DiScioli, Megan Shaw.

Everyone at channel 19 who I've worked with over the years, became friends with, and who taught me many things! Everyone at Tailgate 19 and Fifth Quarter. Chris Arnold, you take such good care of me there! Everyone at Yuengling and House of LaRose who I've worked with the past couple of years. To everyone at the Browns past and present. All Browns alumni. Everyone I've ever worked with over the years, done interviews with. Shaun Robbins, Tom Megalis, Rick Buccheri. Everyone at PFUFA, HOF and J. Babe Stearn Center, especially Tim Haverstock.

To everyone who ever commissioned me to paint or design their space. An extra special thank you to John and Ann Wolfe, Katie and Clark Lloyd, Rita Wolfe, Peggy Fowler and the Fowler family, Vickie Hutchins, JoAnn and Jay Martin, Barb and Joe Webb, Doug and Rosemary Kohler, Gordan and Carole Hyatt, David Drummond. Huge thanks to Billy McClurg Dawgbyte productions, who has done my website since 1999! To my landlords Angela and Andrew Toth! To every guy I've ever dated, thank you for being a mirror for me to learn about myself even if it was painful. To the spirits that walk beside me on my journey especially the Angels, Ancestors, Ascended Masters, Creator, the Earth, Animals who have helped guide me on my path, I'm grateful for all that you show me for we are all connected. I wasn't on my true path until I met all of you. To all of my teachers here on the Earth. Your books, talks, writings, quotes, videos all seem to find me at the moment I need them! Ah, Divine Timing is a beautiful thing! To the musicians who are my soundtrack for life as well as writing this book. Van Morrison, your music is poetry to my heart. To the artists and writers on the other side who have helped guide me with inspiration and whose courage to be themselves I greatly admire and have inspired me to do the same.

We come to the Earth alone and we leave alone but while we are here we never walk alone!

xoxo —Bone

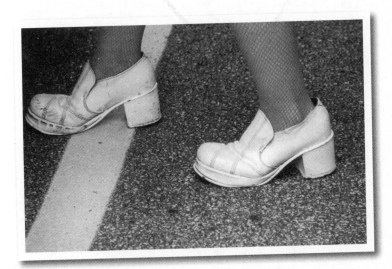